Taste
OF THE
WORLD

Compiled by
FACS (Home Economics) Teachers

Editor
Betty Rabin-Fung

Graphic Design, Typography & Production
Mike Burk Production Services, Long Beach, CA

Visit us at: **www.creativecookbook.com**

ISBN 978-0-9845748-2-7

1/122M062011MBPS/DPS

Thank you for purchasing this book. The sale helps raise much needed money for school programs. We hope you discover wonderful new recipes from around the world. And, a big thanks to the Family & Consumer Science and Home Economics Teachers for donating the quality recipes. Their names are listed in the back index.

TEACHER ADVISORY COMMITTEE

Barbara Allen
Ayala High School, Chino Hills, CA

Patti Bartholomew
Casa Roble High School, Orangevale, CA

Priscilla Burns
Pleasant Valley High School, Chico, CA

Diane Castro
Temecula Valley High School, Temecula, CA

Neva Clauson
Lebanon High School, Lebanon, OR

Diane Cluff
Provo High School, Provo, UT

Jamey Davis
Redwood Int School, Thousand Oaks, CA

Leigh Ann Diffenderfer
Newbury Park High School
Newbury Park, CA

Maria Fregulia
Lassen High School, Susanville, CA

Debbie Harvey
Amador Valley High School
Pleasanton, CA

Camille Hicks
Riverton High School, Riverton, UT

Karyn Hobbs
Lemoore High School, Lemoore, CA

Reiko Ikkanda
So Pasadena Middle School, So Pasadena, CA

Ruth Kerr
State Supervisor, Family & Consumer Sciences
Arizona Department of Education

Mary Lash
Paramount High School, Paramount, CA

Gail McAuley
Lincoln High School, Stockton, CA

Mary Morrow
Mesa High School, Mesa, AZ

Betty Rabin-Fung
Sierra Vista JHS, Canyon Country, CA

Gaylen Roe
Magnolia Junior High School, Chino, CA

Stephanie San Sebastian
Central High School, Fresno, CA

Suzi Schneider
Bret Harte High School, Angels Camp, CA

Anne Silveira
Shasta High School, Redding, CA

Karen Tilson
Poly High School, Riverside, CA

Melissa Webb
California Department of Education
Education Programs Consultant

Thanks to the following people for working hard to provide a good product and a simple, successful fundraiser. We couldn't do it without you!

Betty Rabin-Fung edits each recipe to insure they are error-free. **Sue Russell**, a full-time teacher spends many hours typing, and organizing the recipes. **Ron Cline, Ron Rouintree,** and **Jason Medina** provide excellent customer service.

Tim Campbell, Grady Reed and **Marc Trimble** help the teachers to be successful with their sales. **Mike Burk** oversees the design, layout and production of our books. **Jerry Bernstein** and **Delta Printing Solutions** print and bind our books.

A final thanks to the students who sell these books, helping to improve the quality of the school programs they are involved with.

Sincerely,
Doug Pierce and **Doug Herrema,** owners, **Creative Cookbook Company**

To reorder this and other books, visit our website: **www.creativecookbook.com** or use the re-order form on page 159.

TABLE OF CONTENTS

Curried Pork Kabobs

Serves: 4   *India*

- 1 pound boneless pork loin, cut into 1/2-inch cubes
- 1 cup plain low-fat yogurt
- 2 tablespoons orange juice
- 1 tablespoon ground coriander
- 1/2 teaspoon turmeric
- 1/2 teaspoon ground cumin
- 1/2 teaspoon salt
- 1/4 teaspoon ground ginger

In medium bowl stir together yogurt, orange juice and seasonings; add pork to bowl, stir to coat with marinade. Cover and refrigerate 4-24 hours. Remove pork from marinade; shaking cubes gently to remove excess marinade. Discard remaining marinade. Skewer pork evenly on skewers. Grill over medium-hot fire, turning frequently, for about 10 minutes, until nicely browned.

National Pork Board   PorkBeInspired.com

Africa

• •

African Peanut Soup

Serves: 15-20   *Africa*

3 tablespoons vegetable oil
2 whole onions, diced
3 cloves garlic, minced
1 cup tomato paste
2 cups peanut butter
12 cups chicken stock
3/8 teaspoons cayenne pepper
salt and pepper, to taste
4 cups chicken, diced, optional

In a large saucepan, heat the oil over medium heat. Fry the onions until golden brown, add the garlic and continue to fry for 1 minute more. Remove the pan from the heat. Add tomato paste, peanut butter, and about 1 cup of the broth. Whisk until smooth. Return to medium-low heat and slowly whisk in remaining broth. Simmer, covered, for 10 minutes, stirring occasionally. Add the seasonings, stir and taste. Adjust the salt and pepper; simmer for an additional 10 minutes or until the oil floats to the surface. Skim off the oil. Add the chicken pieces, stir and serve hot.

Maria Nicolaides   Ocean View HS, Huntington Beach, CA

Kwanzaa Chocolate Cake

Serves: 12-16   *Africa*

2/3 cup butter or margarine, softened
1 1/2 cups sugar
1 teaspoon vanilla extract
2 eggs
2 cups all-purpose flour
3/4 cup cocoa powder
1 1/2 teaspoons baking soda
1 teaspoon salt
1 (16 ounce) container dairy sour cream
3/4 cup banana, mashed
1 cup sweetened coconut flakes
1/2 to 1 teaspoon orange peel, freshly grated (optional)
cream cheese frosting
sliced bananas, kiwi fruit and tangerine
Cream Cheese Frosting:
8 ounces cream cheese
1/2 cup butter
2 cups powdered sugar
1/2 cup walnuts or pecans

Preheat oven to 350 degrees. Grease and flour 12-cup fluted tube pan. Beat butter, sugar and vanilla in large bowl until creamy. Beat in eggs. Stir together flour, cocoa, baking soda and salt; add alternately with sour cream to butter mixture, beating until well blended. Stir in bananas, coconut and orange peel. Pour batter into prepared pan. Bake 55-60 minutes or until wooden pick inserted comes out clean. Cool 10 minutes; remove from pan to wire rack. Cool completely. Prepare frosting; spread over whole cake. Garnish with fresh fruits an hour before serving. *Cream Cheese Frosting:* Cream butter and cream cheese together. Mix in powdered sugar until smooth. Sprinkle nuts on top of cake. Arrange fruit on top of cake.

   Alice Claiborne   Fairfield HS, Fairfield, CA

Madagascar Chicken

Serves: 8   *Africa*

1-2 pounds chicken breast, boneless, cut into bite sized chunks
1 cup canned coconut milk
1 onion, chopped
2 red bell peppers or tomatoes, chopped
2 cloves garlic, minced
2 teaspoons ground ginger
1 teaspoon grated lemon rind
1/3 teaspoon cayenne pepper
salt
pepper
lemon juice
oil

Marinate chicken in lemon juice for 30 minutes. Drain and season with salt and pepper to taste. Sauté over medium heat until cooked on outside but still slightly pink inside. Drain oil and place chicken in a container and set aside. Sauté onion until slightly browned. Add bell peppers and garlic and sauté 3-4 minutes, stirring constantly. Reduce heat to simmer, add coconut milk, ginger, cayenne and lemon rind. Add chicken back to stew. Cover and simmer 30 minutes or until thick stew consistency. Serve over steamed rice or ugali.

Patty Bulat   Rogers MS, Long Beach, CA

Mombasa Pumpkin Dessert

Serves: 8   *Africa*

1 (28 ounce) can pureed pumpkin
3 cups sugar
1 (14.5 ounce) can coconut milk
1 1/2 teaspoons ground cardamon

In a medium sauce pan, combine the pumpkin and sugar. Heat over medium - low temperature until sugar dissolves into pumpkin. Add coconut milk and cardamon. Stir often. Cook until mixture has thickened to pudding like consistency.

Janet Hough   Foothill HS, Henderson, NV

Moroccan Glazed Carrots

Serves: 6   *Africa*

12 medium carrots (2 pounds), peeled and ends removed
1/2 tablespoon butter
1/2 tablespoon canola oil
2 tablespoons orange juice
1/2 teaspoon salt
1/4 teaspoon cinnamon
1/4 teaspoon cayenne pepper

Slice carrots to create coin-like pieces. Heat butter and canola oil in a skillet. Add carrots and sauté for 5 minutes. Add rest of the ingredients. Cook until carrots are tender and liquid is absorbed, about 15 minutes. Helpful hints: Cut carrots into pieces of the same size to cook more evenly.

"Everyone loves the spicy flavor. Students share this recipe with their families!"

Diane Scott   Lawrence Jones MS, Rohnert Park, CA

Americana

Artichoke Appetizer

Serves: 6-8   **USA**

1 (6 ounce) jar marinated artichoke hearts
1 (8 ounce) package cream cheese, room temperature
1 (6 ounce) block parmesan cheese, grated
1/4 teaspoon dill weed
1 cup mayonnaise
garlic salt, to taste

Preheat oven to 350 degrees. Drain and chop artichoke hearts. Blend cream cheese, parmesan cheese, dill, garlic salt and mayonnaise. Stir in artichokes. Bake uncovered, in a buttered (or greased) quart dish for 20 minutes until browned and bubbly. Serve hot with crackers, chips or bread.

"This is a request at every party - I'm not invited in if I don't bring it! Easy and so good!"

Beth Leighton   **Helix Charter HS, La Mesa, CA**

BBQ Chicken Pizza

Serves: 3-4   **USA**

1 prepared pizza crust (I like Boboli)
1/2 cup barbecue sauce (I like Sweet Baby Ray's)
3 cups grated mozzarella cheese
1 cup cooked chicken, cut into bite-sized pieces
1/4 cup chopped red onion
1/4 cup chopped cilantro

Preheat oven to 400 degrees. Place pizza crust on a baking sheet and spread with the barbecue sauce. Top the crust with the cheese and then the chicken. Sprinkle the red onion and cilantro over the pizza. Bake in a preheated oven for 12-15 minutes until the cheese is bubbling and the crust is browned. Slice and serve.

"If you are a fan of the BBQ Chicken Pizza at the California Pizza Kitchen, this is a great "copycat" recipe. If you like to make your own pizza crust - prepare it, shape and prebake it for 8 minutes until lightly browned, and then proceed with the recipe."

Beth Guerrero   **Selma HS, Selma, CA**

Blueberry Pizza

Serves: 12   USA

Crust:
1 cup flour
1/4 cup powdered sugar
1/2 cup margarine
Sauce:
5 tablespoons corn starch
4 tablespoons cool water
3 cups blueberries, mashed
1 cup sugar
Cream Filling:
4 ounces cream cheese
1 teaspoon vanilla
3/4 cup powdered sugar
Optional Topping:
4 cups fresh blueberries.

Preheat oven to 325 degrees. Crust: Mix together flour, powdered sugar and margarine. Pat into 12 inch pizza pan. Bake for 10-12 minutes or until slightly brown. Cool. Sauce: Make a paste out of the corn starch and water. Combine paste with mashed blueberries and sugar. Cook on medium heat until mixture is kind of clear and thick. Cool completely. Cheese Filling: Cream together the cream cheese, vanilla and powdered sugar until smooth. Spread over cool crust. Pour cool blueberry sauce over cream cheese filling. Optional Topping: If fresh blueberries are available top sauce with 4 cups of fresh blueberries.

"Other fruits can be used too. Frozen mixed berries are especially good.
Different combinations of fresh fruit can be placed on top as desired.
It is easy to double the recipe and prepare in a 9 x 13 inch pan for easy travel to picnics."

Neva Clausen   Lebanon HS, Lebanon, OR

California Cheesy Potato Soup

Makes: 1 1/2 quarts   USA

4 large potatoes, scrubbed well
2/3 cup butter
2/3 cup flour
1 1/2 quarts milk
4 green onions, chopped
1 cup sour cream
1 pound bacon, cooked & crumbled
8 ounces cheddar cheese, grated
salt and pepper, to taste

Heat oven to 350 degrees. Bake potatoes until tender. In large pot, melt butter, then stir in flour with whisk until blended. Gradually add milk, whisking constantly. Stir in salt and pepper. Cut potatoes in half, scoop out and reserve scooped-out insides. Chop 1/2 of the potato skins; discard or put remaining peels aside for another use. Whisk scooped-out potato into milk mixture, then stir in chopped peels and green onion. Stir in sour cream and bacon, then add cheese a handful at a time until melted.

"Serve with tossed salad and crusty bread for a satisfying meal."

Linda Bejaran   Turlock HS, Turlock, CA

Chocolate Chip Meringue Drops

Makes: 36   **USA**

2 egg whites
1/2 cup white sugar
1 teaspoon vanilla extract
3 tablespoons unsweetened cocoa powder
1/2 cup semisweet chocolate chips

Preheat oven to 250 degrees. Line 2 baking sheets with aluminum foil or parchment paper and set aside. In a large metal or glass bowl, beat the egg whites on high speed with an electric mixer until soft peaks form. Gradually add sugar while continuing to beat until they hold stiff peaks. Mix in the vanilla and cocoa on low speed, then fold in chocolate chips by hand. Drop small mounds of the mixture onto the prepared baking sheets, spacing 1 inch apart. Bake for 1 hour in the preheated oven. Turn off oven, and leave the cookies in the oven for 2 more hours, or until centers are dry. Remove from pan and store in an airtight container. Cookies can be left overnight in the oven. Add 1/4 cup finely chopped pecans for added nutrients as a variation.

"Makes a great gift in a holiday tin."

Maryjo Timmons   Palo Verde HS, Las Vegas, NV

Jessie's Ranch Cheez-its

Makes: 12 cups   **USA**

1 tablespoon dill weed
1 package dry Hidden Valley Ranch dressing mix
3/4 cup oil
2 boxes of Cheez-its crackers

Mix ingredients together and pour over 2 boxes of Cheez-its. Stir often so oil absorbs evenly into crackers.

"A great party food or flavored snack. This was made by a student of mine who brought it often to class to share with their table group."

Jeanette Atkinson   Legacy HS, North Las Vegas, NV

Marinated Carrots

Makes: a lot!   **USA**

1/2 cup sugar
1 teaspoon dry mustard
1 teaspoon salt
1 teaspoon pepper
1 (10.5 ounce) can tomato soup
1/2 cup cider vinegar
1/2 cup vegetable oil
2 1/2 pounds carrots, sliced and cooked
3 green onions, chopped or 1 small white onion, chopped

Mix all ingredients together. Marinate at least 24 hours before serving. Store in a glass jar in the refrigerator.

"A classic recipe from one of the best cooks I know, Angie Nissen!"

Maria Montemagni   Redwood HS, Visalia, CA

Natillas (Boiled Custard)

Serves: 6   USA

4 eggs, separated
1 cup sugar
4 tablespoons flour
1/2 teaspoon salt
4 cups milk
2 teaspoons vanilla
cinnamon

Beat egg whites until stiff. Beat egg yolks, add sugar, flour and salt. Heat the milk, pour egg whites into hot milk, being careful that milk does not boil over. When egg whites are cooked, skim off from milk and place into a serving bowl. Add the egg yolk mixture to the hot milk. (Add a small amount of the hot milk to the yolk mixture to temper the eggs), then add to the milk mixture. Cook for 10 minutes. Pour into the bowl with the egg whites. Fold in the mixture gently. Sprinkle the top with cinnamon. Serve warm or cool in the refrigerator.

"This recipe came from my mother-in law who was from New Mexico.
It is one of my husband's favorite desserts."

Lori Chavez   Mountain View HS, El Monte, CA

Perfect Potato Latkes

Makes: 15-20   USA

4 cups Russet potatoes, peeled and shredded
1 cup onion, grated
1 egg beaten
1 teaspoon salt
2 tablespoons flour
vegetable oil for frying

*Water to soak the potatoes (optional). You can soak the grated potatoes in tap water to keep them from turning brown. If you do this you must thoroughly dry them with a cheesecloth or clean kitchen towel before you mix with the other ingredients.

In a large bowl, add the grated onion, peeled and grated potatoes, beaten egg, salt and flour. Stir gently with fingers. Drop a large spoonful of the mixture into hot oil in a frying pan. Fry both sides until a beautiful golden brown. Enjoy!

"Potato pancakes (or latkes) are the most popular and traditional food served during Hanukkah. Best when crispy. Top with a dollop of sour cream and/or applesauce."

Su Garrett   Grace Yokley MS, Ontario, CA

Pistachio Pudding Salad

Serves: 6-8   USA

1 (3.4 ounce) package instant pistachio pudding
1 (20 ounce) can crushed pineapple
1 (8 ounce) container Cool Whip
1 cup mini marshmallows

Sprinkle pudding over pineapple and beat till thick. Fold in Cool Whip and mini marshmallows with rubber spatula. Optional: Top with crushed walnuts for garnish.

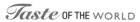
Taste OF THE WORLD

Best to let sit in refrigerator for a few hours or overnight before serving *The Pistachio is an evergreen tree native to Western Asia/Asia Minor.

"This is a festive, sweet salad that is fun to serve during the winter holidays."

Sue Fullmer   ECTA, Las Vegas, NV

Rhubarb Sprinkle Dessert

Serves: 12   **USA**

4 cups fresh rhubarb, coarsely chopped
1 (3 ounce) package strawberry flavored gelatin dessert mix
1 cup granulated sugar
1 cup water
1 (18.25 ounce) package yellow cake mix
1/2 cup coconut
1/2 cup nuts, chopped
3/4 cup melted butter, do not substitute

Preheat oven to 325 degrees. Sprinkle ingredients in a greased 13 x 9 inch baking dish in order listed. Do not mix. Bake until rhubarb is tender 25-35 minutes. Serve warm. Refrigerate any leftovers.

"This a favorite and very easy to make. Good served with a scoop of ice cream or topping."

Jeanette Atkinson   Legacy HS, North Las Vegas, NV

Slow Cooker White Chicken Chili

Makes: 6 quarts   **USA**

3-4 large chicken breasts, trimmed of fat
2 (14 ounce) cans chicken broth
2 teaspoons ground cumin
2 teaspoons dried oregano leaves
1 teaspoon salt
3 cloves garlic, minced
1 teaspoon crushed red pepper
1 (15 ounce) can white shoe peg corn, drained
2 (15 ounce) cans white beans (white kidneys, great northern, whatever), drained
2 tablespoons fresh cilantro, chopped
3 tablespoons lime juice

Add chicken, broth, cumin, oregano, salt, garlic, and red pepper to your slow cooker. Cover and cook on low for 6-8 hours or until chicken falls apart. Shred the chicken into medium sized chunks with two forks. Drain and rinse the corn and beans and add them to the slow cooker. Add cilantro and lime juice. Put cover back on and cook for 30 more minutes or until heated through.

"This recipe comes from my cousin who is a domestic queen. Thanks Jenny! Served with cornbread this chili recipe is fit for any occasion."

Katie Borgmeier   Riverton HS, Riverton, UT

Texas Sheet Cake

Serves: 8-10   **USA**

2 cups flour
2 cups sugar
1 teaspoon baking soda
1/2 teaspoon salt
1/2 cup sour cream
2 eggs
1 cup butter
1 cup water
5 tablespoons unsweetened cocoa powder
Frosting:
6 tablespoons milk
5 tablespoons unsweetened cocoa powder
1/2 cup butter
4 cups confectioners sugar
1 teaspoon vanilla

Preheat oven to 350 degrees. Grease and flour a 10 x 15 inch sheet pan. Combine flour, sugar, baking soda and salt; beat in the sour cream and eggs. Set aside. Melt butter on low in a saucepan, add water and cocoa. Bring to a boil, then remove from heat. Allow to cool slightly, then pour in small amounts into the batter mixture and beat until blended. Pour batter into prepared pan and bake in the preheated oven for 20 minutes or until a toothpick comes out clean. *Frosting:* While cake is cooling; In a large sauce pan, combine the milk, cocoa and butter. Bring to a boil then remove from heat. Stir in the sugar and vanilla. Mix until blended. Spread frosting over warm cake.

"This is a family favorite. It is also easy and quick to prepare."

Linda Brayton   **Grace Davis HS, Modesto, CA**

Zucchini Casserole

Serves: 12 Depending on size of cuts   **USA**

3 1/2 cups zucchini, thinly sliced
1/2 cup onion, chopped (I like to use red onions),
1 clove garlic
1 cup Bisquick
1/2 cup oil
1/2 teaspoon marjoram (seasoning)
1/4 teaspoon season salt
1/2 cup Parmesan cheese
4 eggs, slightly beaten

Preheat oven to 350 degrees. Combine all ingredients in large bowl. Pour into greased 9 x 13 inch baking dish and top with paprika. Bake for 30 to 45 minutes.

"Another winner using Zucchini from my Mother-in-law's cards. A great dish to serve as a side with lunch, dinner, or to take on a picnic. Can be either served hot or cold."

Dianne Lee Goldman   **Cordova HS, Rancho Cordova, CA**

Maryland Crab Cakes

Makes: 5-6   **USA Mid-Atlantic**

6 saltine crackers, crushed to fine crumbs
1/2 pound crab meat
1 egg
2 tablespoons mayonnaise
1 teaspoon lemon juice, freshly squeezed
1 teaspoon Worcestershire sauce
dash hot sauce, such as Tabasco
1/4 teaspoon salt
1/4 teaspoon pepper
2 tablespoons peanut oil

In a large bowl, gently mix together all of the ingredients, except oil. The mixture will be wet. Form into 4-5 small patties of equivalent size. Heat peanut oil in a medium nonstick skillet over medium heat. Gently slide the cakes off a spatula into the oil. Cook about 3 at a time. Sauté until the crab cakes are golden brown and cooked through, about 4-5 minutes on each side. Remove from skillet and drain on paper towels. Serve hot with tartar or cocktail sauce, if desired. Variations: You can add 1-2 teaspoons Old Bay seasoning, 1 teaspoon dry mustard, and extra dash of Worcestershire sauce, or 1 1/2 tablespoons finely chopped parsley. You can use fine, fresh bread crumbs as a coating instead.

"This recipe is becoming more and more popular as students are appreciating seafood."
    DeeAnn Verdi   McQueen HS, Reno, NV

Caramel Rolls

Serves: 6-8   **USA Midwest**

1 package yeast
1 teaspoon sugar
1/4 cup warm water
1 teaspoon salt
2 tablespoons sugar
1 cup milk
2 tablespoons butter
1 egg
3 1/2 cups flour
1 cube margarine
2 tablespoons milk
3/4 cup brown sugar
cinnamon and sugar to sprinkle over dough

Preheat oven to 350. In a small bowl, combine yeast, sugar and warm water. Set aside. In a large bowl, add salt and 2 tablespoons sugar. Set aside. In a saucepan, heat milk and 2 tablespoons butter. After milk cools a bit, add beaten egg. Add yeast sugar water from the small bowl. Combine. Pour contents into the large bowl and add flour. Work dough with a spoon; should be elastic. Cover and let rise. To make caramel: Add margarine cube, milk and brown sugar to a saucepan. Heat then cool until melted and thick. After the dough rises, work dough again and let rest for 15 to 20 minutes. Spread out to 1/2 inch thick. Roll dough into log shape. Cut into 1/2 inch rolls after sprinkling with cinnamon and sugar. Put caramel mixture into the bottom of a 9 x 13 pan. Place rolls on top of caramel mixture. Bake for 25 to 30 minutes. Turn out to serve.

"My Aunt Bev from Wisconsin made these when she visited our home. So delicious!"

Julie Eyre   Alhambra HS, Alhambra, CA

Chicken Creamette Casserole

Serves: 6-8   *USA Midwest*

2 cups cooked chicken, diced
2 (10.5 ounce) cream of mushroom soup
2 cups milk
1 (12 ounce) package uncooked macaroni
1 small onion, chopped
1/2 pound Velveeta or American cheese, shredded
1 (4 ounce) jar pimiento, diced
crushed potato chips

Mix together lightly all ingredients (except potato chips) in 9 X 13 inch pan. Refrigerate overnight. Top with crushed potato chips and bake 1 hour at 350 degrees. Two cans of tuna or diced ham may be substituted for the chicken.

"You can make it ahead of time and don't have to cook the macaroni first."

Monica Blanchette   Landmark MS, Moreno Valley, CA

Nana's Pasties

Serves: 4   *USA Midwest*

1 (15 ounce) package All Ready Pie Crusts
1 pound flank steak, finely chopped
3 large potatoes, peeled and cubed
1 large turnip, peeled and cubed
1 large onion, chopped
1 teaspoon salt
1 teaspoon pepper
1/4 teaspoon garlic powder

Preheat oven to 350 degrees. Combine all ingredients including spices in large mixing bowl. Roll dough into 4 - 6 inch circles and place 1 cup of combined ingredients on one side of dough and fold calzone style (pinch edges or flute to seal). Repeat and place on greased cookie sheet. Bake for 25-30 minutes. Serve warm or cold.

"Pasties remind me of my grandmother; she would make these meat pies and the whole family would head to Champion Beach for a picnic. Great cold with ketchup."

Linda Bejaran   Turlock HS, Turlock, CA

Jambalaya

Serves: 4-6   ***USA New Orleans/Cajun***

1/2 medium onion, small diced
1/4 green bell pepper, small diced
2 celery stalks, small diced
1 carrot, finely diced
1/2 pound smoked Cajun sausage
1 (14 1/2 ounce) can diced tomatoes plus 3 cans water
3/4 cup tomato sauce
1 tablespoon chicken bouillon base
3/4 cup long grain rice, uncooked but rinsed
1/2 teaspoon salt
1/2 teaspoon thyme
1/2 teaspoon cayenne pepper
1/2 teaspoon chili powder
1/2 teaspoon sugar
1/8 teaspoon hot sauce, optional
1 teaspoon dried parsley flakes (or 1 tablespoon fresh)
1/2 pound shrimp

Chop onion and pepper into 1/4 inch dice. Peel carrot and cut into 1/8 inch dice. Mince garlic. Rinse rice. Slice 1/4 inch thick slices of sausage and sauté in a large pot with oil. Brown sausage slightly on both side over medium heat, remove to a plate temporarily. Add vegetables and cook for about 3 minutes. Stir in can of diced tomatoes plus water, tomato sauce, bouillon base, rice, salt, thyme, cayenne pepper, chili powder and sugar. Bring to a boil, cover and reduce to a simmer for 20 minutes or until rice is tender. Stir periodically checking to see if additional water is needed. Stir in parsley, shrimp and cooked sausage and cook an additional 8-10 minutes. Add additional hot sauce as needed.

"This is always a favorite. I have students who take my class asking about this dish, they had sampled it from a friend who had taken the class a previous year."
DeeAnn Verdi   McQueen HS, Reno, NV

Puffy French Toast

Makes: About 8 servings   ***USA New Orleans/Cajun***

1 cup flour, sifted
1 1/2 teaspoons sugar
1 1/2 teaspoons baking powder
1/2 teaspoon salt
1/4 teaspoon cinnamon
1 egg, beaten
1 cup milk
vegetable oil for deep frying
8 slices of white bread (I use small slices of sourdough)

Stir together dry ingredients. Beat egg into milk and stir into dry ingredients to form batter. Heat enough oil in a skillet to cover a slice of bread, half way up. Dip one slice of bread into batter, cover both sides with batter. Carefully place battered bread into hot oil and fry until golden and puffed. Flip bread over and repeat until both sides are golden. Serve with butter and syrup or fresh fruit and powdered sugar.

"This makes a great presentation and always gets rave reviews!"

Carol Pellet   Sowers MS, Huntington Beach, CA

Corn Chowder

Serves: 8   **USA Northeast**

6 ears fresh corn, cut from cob (save the cobs, will use when simmering soup)
2 (15 ounce) cans whole kernel corn, drained
   (use Del Monte fresh cut Golden Sweet Corn)
5 cups low sodium chicken broth
3 slices bacon, chopped fine
1 onion, chopped
salt and pepper
1 pound red potatoes (about 4) scrubbed and cut into 1/2 inch dice
1/2 cup heavy cream
4 scallions, sliced thin

Cut kernels from ears of corn; reserve kernels and cobs separately. Puree canned corn and 2 cups of the broth in blender until smooth. Cook bacon in Dutch oven over medium heat until crisp, about 8 minutes. Using slotted spoon, transfer bacon to paper towel lined plate and reserve. Cook onion, corn kernels, 1/2 teaspoon salt and 1/4 teaspoon pepper in bacon fat until vegetables are softened and golden brown, 6-8 minutes. Add potatoes, corn puree, remaining broth and reserved corn cobs to Dutch oven and bring to boil. Reduce heat to medium-low and simmer until potatoes are tender, about 15 minutes. Discard cobs and stir in cream, scallions and reserved cooked bacon, season with salt and pepper. (I don't think it needs anymore salt.) Enjoy! Soup can be refrigerated in airtight container for up to 3 days.

"This old fashioned corn chowder simmers with the entire cob for incredible flavor."

Adriana Molinaro   Granite Hills HS, El Cajon, CA

Cranberry Apple Crisp

Serves: 8   **USA Pacific Northwest**

5 medium tart apples, sliced
1 tablespoon flour
1 (16 ounce) can whole berry cranberry sauce
Topping:
3/4 cup quick cooking oats
1/3 cup packed brown sugar
1/4 cup all purpose flour
2 tablespoons canola oil
2 tablespoons butter, melted
3/4 teaspoon cinnamon

Preheat oven to 350 degrees. In a large bowl, combine apples and flour, toss to coat. Stir in cranberry sauce. Transfer to a 9 x 13 inch pan coated with cooking spray. In a small bowl, combine topping ingredients; sprinkle over apple mixture. Bake, uncovered for 40-45 minutes or until topping is golden brown and fruit is tender.

"A new family favorite . Lighter and so, so good."

Jan Runyan   Palm Desert Charter MS, Palm Desert, CA

Black-eyed Pea Fritters

Makes: 72   *USA Southern*

2 cups black-eyed peas, dried
1 1/2 cups onion, diced
1 tablespoon jalapeno pepper, diced
2 large whole eggs
2 teaspoons salt
6-8 tablespoons water
vegetable oil to fry
Relish:
3 pounds red bell peppers, diced
2 whole onions, diced fine
4 plum tomatoes, diced
2 tablespoons jalapeno pepper
1 tablespoon salt
1/2 cup peanut oil

Soak the peas in water to cover by 2 inches for 8 hours. Drain in a colander. To make the relish, prepare the vegetables. Puree the bell pepper, onion, tomatoes, pepper and salt in two batches in the food processor. Heat oil in a large fry pan over medium heat until oil is hot, but not smoking. Gradually stir in the pureed vegetables, turn down heat and simmer until most of the liquid evaporates (about 10 minutes) while stirring. Remove from heat and cool. Puree the black-eyed peas, onion and pepper in food processor until as smooth as possible, blend in eggs and salt. With the processor running, add 6 tablespoons of water and blend until smooth and fluffy. Add more water, if necessary, to form a batter just thin enough to drop from a spoon. Heat oil to 360 degrees. Working in batches of 8, gently drop tablespoons of batter into the hot oil. Fry, using a slotted spoon to stir constantly to prevent browning too quickly, until the fritters are golden brown (about 2 minutes). Drain on absorbent paper. Serve hot.

Maria Nicolaides   Ocean View HS, Huntington Beach, CA

Collard Greens

Serves: 8   *USA Southern*

1 brown onion, diced
2 generous slices ham, turkey ham, diced OR 6 slices bacon, cooked and crumbled
1/4 cup olive oil
2 tablespoons hot pepper flakes
2 or 3 cloves garlic, pressed
2 bunches collard greens, cleaned
1 head of cabbage, sliced
salt and pepper, to taste

Sauté onions, ham or bacon, garlic, and pepper flakes in olive oil until hot and cooked soft in large 4 quart pot over medium heat. Add cleaned, wet, collard greens and sliced cabbage to pot and turn heat to low. Cover and cook for about 30 min. until cooked through. Add salt and pepper to taste before serving.

"I guess that adding cabbage to collard greens helps to "northernize" the recipe and blends my Minnesota roots to my husband's Texas roots."

Monica Blanchette   Landmark MS, Moreno Valley, CA

Cornbread

Serves: 4-6   **USA Southern**

1 egg
1 cup biscuit mix (Bisquick)
1/2 cup milk
1/4 cup oil
1/4 teaspoon baking soda
1/3 cup sugar
2 tablespoons cornmeal

Preheat oven to 375 degrees. Slightly beat egg and stir in with milk and oil. Measure dry ingredients into a bowl. Add in liquid ingredients and mix well. Pour into a greased loaf pan. Bake for 20 minutes.

"Great with soups."

LeeAnn Bitner   Alta HS, Sandy, UT

French Apple Cobbler

Serves: 6   **USA Southern**

Apple Filling:
5 cups tart apples, peeled, sliced (about 5-6 apples)
3/4 cup sugar or brown sugar
2 tablespoons flour
1/2 teaspoon cinnamon
1/4 teaspoon salt
1 teaspoon vanilla extract
1/4 cup water
1 tablespoon butter, softened
Topping:
1/2 cup flour
1/2 cup sugar
1/2 teaspoon baking powder
1/4 teaspoon salt
2 tablespoons butter, softened
1 egg, slightly beaten

Preheat oven to 375 degrees. Filling: In a medium bowl, combine apples, sugar, flour, cinnamon, salt, vanilla and water. Turn into a lightly buttered 9-inch square pan. Dot apples with butter. Combine all topping ingredients. Beat with wooden spoon until batter is smooth. Drop batter in 9 portions, over the apples, spacing evenly. Batter will spread during baking. Bake for 35-40 minutes or until apples are tender and crust is golden brown.

"I found this recipe online when I was looking for "Southern Food" recipes last year. It was a hit with my students and family."

Michelle Baker   Kern Valley HS, Lake Isabella, CA

Red Velvet Cake

Serves: 8   **USA Southern**

Red Velvet Cake:
1/2 cup shortening
1 1/2 cups sugar
2 eggs
2 ounces red food coloring
1 cup buttermilk
2 1/4 cups flour
1 teaspoon salt
1 teaspoon vanilla
1 teaspoon baking soda
1 teaspoon vinegar
Red Velvet Frosting:
3 tablespoons flour
1 cup milk
1 cup sugar
1 teaspoon vanilla
1 cup butter

Preheat oven to 350 degrees. Cream shortening, sugar, and eggs together, add food coloring, add buttermilk, alternating with flour and salt, add vanilla, add soda to vinegar; blend into batter. Pour into 2 (8 inch) or 2 (9 inch) cake pans that have been greased and floured. Bake for 24-30 minutes. Red Velvet Frosting: Cook flour and milk until thick, stirring constantly. Cool completely. Cream sugar, butter, and vanilla together; add to cooled cooked mixture. Beat on high speed until fluffy. A very special frosting for a very special cake.

"My mother was from the south and would bake this cake for special occasions. The frosting recipe is very different but delicious. It is so much better then the cream cheese frosting that is being used on Red Velvet cakes today."

Wendy Duncan   **West Covina HS, West Covina, CA**

Sweet Potato Casserole

Serves: 12   **USA Southern**

2 (29 ounce) cans sweet potatoes
1/2 cup sugar
1/2 cup butter
2 eggs, beaten
1 teaspoon vanilla
1/3 cup evaporated milk
Topping:
1/3 cup melted butter
1 cup light brown sugar
1/2 cup flour
1 cup pecans, chopped

Preheat oven to 350 degrees. Heat both cans of sweet potatoes to boiling, drain and then mash. Mix sugar, butter, eggs, vanilla and milk into the hot potatoes. Put into a casserole dish. Topping: Melt butter and mix in remaining ingredients. Sprinkle on top of potato mixture and bake for about 35 minutes or until the topping is golden brown.

"Even those who don't like sweet potatoes enjoy this! It's a dessert disguised as a side dish."

Jeanette Neese   **Enterprise HS, Redding, CA**

Black and Garbanzo Bean Soup

Serves: 4   **USA Southwest**

1 tablespoon olive oil
1 small white onion, chopped
1 tablespoon chili powder
1 teaspoon ground cumin
1 (15 ounce) can black beans, rinsed
1 (15 ounce) can garbanzo beans, rinsed
3 cups water
1/2 cup prepared salsa (your favorite)
1/4 teaspoon salt
1 tablespoon lime juice
4 tablespoons reduced-fat sour cream (optional)
2 tablespoons fresh cilantro, chopped

Add oil and onion to a medium saucepan over medium heat. Cook, stirring, until beginning to soften, about 2 to 3 minutes. Add chili powder and cumin and cook stirring, 1 minute more. Add black beans and garbanzo beans, water, salsa and salt. Bring to a boil; reduce heat and simmer for 10 minutes. Remove from the heat and stir in lime juice. Transfer half the soup to a blender and puree (use caution when pureeing hot liquids). Stir the puree back into the saucepan. Serve garnished with sour cream and cilantro. Use 2 cans of black beans if you don't care for garbanzo beans.

"Quick, easy, delicious USA Southwestern-flavor. Satisfying low-calorie dinner with a tossed green salad and whole-grain baguette. Soup lovers are going to love this recipe!"

Brenda Burke   **Mt. Whitney HS, Visalia, CA**

Black Bean Salsa

Serves: 6   **USA Southwest**

1 (15 ounce) can black beans, drained and rinsed
1 cup of tomatoes, seeded and diced
1/2 cup red onion, slivered
1/4 cup cilantro, minced
2 tablespoons jalapeno, seeded and minced
1 tablespoon fresh lime juice
1 tablespoon olive oil

Black Bean Salsa: Combine all ingredients in a bowl, tossing well to coat. Chill salsa until ready to serve.

"Great served over Tortilla Soup as a garnish."

Donna DeWitz   **Oakmont HS, Roseville, CA**

21

Chipotle Chicken Taco Salad

Serves: 8   **USA Southwest**

Salad:
4 cups Romaine lettuce, chopped
2 cups shredded chicken (canned or cooked and shredded)
1 (15 ounce) can black beans, rinsed and drained
1 (15 ounce) can shoe peg corn, rinsed and drained
1 cup cherry/grape tomatoes or diced tomatoes
1/3 cup red onions, sliced
1 avocado, cubed
tortilla strips
Dressing:
1/3 cup fresh cilantro, chopped
2/3 cup sour cream (or Ranch dressing)
1 1/2 teaspoons Chipotle seasoning
1 teaspoon Chili powder
4 teaspoons lime juice (fresh is best)
pinch of salt

Combine lettuce, chicken, black beans, corn, onion and tomatoes in large bowl and gently mix with your hands. Set aside. Mix dressing ingredients. When ready to serve add avocado, tortilla strips and dressing. Mix gently.

"I got this recipe from my daughter. It is a healthy and easy meal that tastes great."

Camille Hicks   Riverton HS, Riverton, UT

Fiesta Corn Chowder

Serves: 6-8   **USA Southwest**

1/2 cup carrots, finely chopped
1/2 cup celery, finely chopped
1 (14.5 ounce) can chicken broth
1 (14.5 ounce) can creamed corn
1 (14.5 ounce) can whole kernel corn, drained
2 cups chicken, finely diced
1 teaspoon to 1 tablespoon jalapeno chile, diced
salt and pepper, to taste
1/2 cup half & half
2 potatoes, peeled and diced small
bacon bits, for garnish
3 corn tortillas, sliced in strips and fried, for garnish

In a large saucepan, cook carrots and celery in chicken broth until tender. Add corn, chicken, jalapeno, salt, pepper, half & half and potatoes. Simmer 30 to 40 minutes, stirring frequently to avoid sticking. Garnish with bacon bits and tortilla chips. Serve piping hot. Flavor will be enhanced if prepared and refrigerated for 24 hours before serving.

Carrie Smith   Royal HS, Simi Valley, CA

Honey Lime Chicken Enchiladas

Serves: 6-8   **USA Southwest**

4 - 6 tablespoons honey
5 tablespoons lime juice (1 or 2 limes)
1 tablespoon chili powder (sprinkle on chicken)
1/2 teaspoon garlic powder
1 pound chicken, cooked and shredded (about 3 chicken breasts)
8 -10 flour tortillas
1 pound Monterey Jack cheese, shredded
16 ounces green enchilada sauce
1 cup heavy cream

Mix the first four ingredients and toss with shredded chicken. Let it marinate for at least 1/2 hour. Preheat oven to 350 degrees. Spray bottom of a 9 x 13 inch pan with vegetable oil. Pour 1/2 cup enchilada sauce on the bottom of the pan. Fill flour tortillas with chicken (save the marinade for sauce) and shredded cheese (save about 1 cup to sprinkle on top of enchiladas). Mix the remaining enchilada sauce with the cream and left over marinade. Pour sauce on top of the enchiladas and sprinkle with cheese. Bake for 20-30 minutes until brown and crispy on top.

"This is a wonderful recipe my daughter found.
It also freezes well for a quick meal you can make ahead."

Camille Hicks   **Riverton HS, Riverton, UT**

Mexicorn Salad

Serves: 12   **USA Southwest**

2 (15 ounce) cans corn, drained
2 (11 ounce) cans mexicorn, drained (has to be this, can't be the
    USA Southwest style or anything else)
1 red bell pepper, chopped about as small as the corn
1 green pepper, chopped (same as above)
6 green onions, chopped
2 cups shredded sharp cheddar
1 1/2 cups mayonnaise
1 bag chili cheese Fritos, crushed

Combine all ingredients, except chips, in a large bowl. Chill for several hours or overnight. Add and combine chips just before serving. Use right away. The chips get soggy in the fridge, so half the recipe if you won't use it all at once.

"This is another great recipe that my cousin passed along to me."

Katie Borgmeier   **Riverton HS, Riverton, UT**

Papa's Eggs

Serves: 4   **USA Southwest**

1/4 cup vegetable oil
3-4 corn tortillas, cut into 1/8ths
1/2 cup onion, diced
1 clove garlic, minced
1 tomato, seeded, diced
6 eggs, well beaten
1/2 cup salsa
salt and pepper, to taste

In a large nonstick skillet, heat oil. Fry corn tortilla pieces until very crisp. Remove and drain; set aside. In a small skillet, sauté onion, garlic and tomatoes until onion is clear and tender. Remove and set aside. In the same skillet, scramble eggs until just done; don't overcook. Add tortilla pieces, onion, garlic and tomato mixture and salsa to the eggs. Heat through. Season to taste with salt and pepper. Serve immediately.

"This is a great recipe to prepare at school because it's easy and the students love it. For a spicy flavor, add 1 1/2 teaspoons red pepper flakes."

Diane Castro   **Temecula Valley HS, Temecula, CA**

Salmon, Black Beans and Rice

Serves: 4   **USA Southwest**

    2 cups brown rice
    1 pound salmon fillets, fresh or frozen
    1 (15 ounce) can tomatoes (any kind, including with chili, herbs, Rotel, etc.)
    1 (15 ounce) can black beans

Preheat oven to 350 degrees. Bring 4 cups water to a boil in a large saucepan. When water reaches the boiling point, add 2 cups of brown rice; return to boil, then reduce heat to low and cook until water is absorbed, about 45 minutes. Cut a large sheet of aluminum foil. Lay salmon on foil. Open can of tomatoes (drain slightly, if desired) and put on top. Open can of black beans, rinse and put on top. Seal foil, then place packet in a pan in case the juices run out. Bake for 30 minutes. Serve salmon over half of the rice (freeze the extra to save time on another night). Notes: To save even more time, use instant brown rice, which cooks in about 10 minutes. For variations, try using peach or mango salsa instead of the tomatoes. Or use the same basic method, but with pork chops and canned fruit salad.

"Often requested recipe from Lynda Spann, CCSD, Las Vegas, NV."

Sue Fullmer   **ECTA, Las Vegas, NV**

Taco Soup

Serves: 6-8   **USA Southwest**

    1 pound hamburger
    1 medium onion, diced
    2 cloves garlic, minced
    1 (1 ounce) package taco seasoning
    1 (16 ounce) can diced tomatoes & juice
    1 (16 ounce) can tomato sauce
    1 (6 ounce) can tomato paste
    1 (16 ounce) can olives, chopped
    1 (16 ounce) can pinto beans
    1 (16 ounce) can whole kernel corn

Brown meat with onion and garlic in a soup pot. Pour off any fat. Add taco seasoning, stirring thoroughly. Add remaining ingredients and cook for 30 to 45 minutes. Serve with Scoop Fritos, grated cheese, sour cream and avocado. Yum!

Gail McAuley   **Lincoln HS, Stockton, CA**

Tortilla Soup

Serves: 6 servings   ***USA Southwest***
2 tablespoons olive oil
1 1/2 cups yellow onion, diced
2 tablespoons garlic, minced
3 corn tortillas cut into 1-inch pieces
1 (10 ounce) can diced tomatoes with green chilies
4 cups chicken broth
1 teaspoon ground cumin
1 teaspoon ground coriander
1/2 teaspoon cayenne pepper
4 boneless, skinless chicken breasts, poached and shredded
1 1/2 cups frozen corn kernels
1/2 cup heavy cream
1 cup Monterey jack cheese, shredded
2 tablespoons fresh lime juice
salt and pepper to taste
Black Bean Salsa
sour cream

Heat oil in stockpot over medium-high; add onions and garlic, and sauté 3 minutes. Stir in tortilla pieces and sauté until they are no longer crisp. Add tomatoes, broth, and spices, then bring to a boil. Remove from heat; let cool 5 minutes, then puree soup base in batches in a blender or food processor until smooth. Return to stockpot. Add chicken, corn, and cream. Bring to a boil, reduce heat and simmer 5 minutes or until beginning to thicken. Sprinkle in cheese and stir until melted. Add lime juice and season with salt and pepper to taste. Garnish with black bean salsa (recipe also in book) and sour cream.

"Our Advanced Culinary class prepared and served this soup at our on-campus student-run cafe, it was a hit with all the patrons!"
    Donna DeWitz   Oakmont HS, Roseville, CA

White Bean Chili

Serves: 12   ***USA Southwest***
4 chicken breasts, boneless, shredded
1 medium onion, chopped
1 (30 ounce) can Las Palmas Enchilada Green Sauce
1 (4 ounce) can diced green chile
1 (15 ounce) jar Herdez Green Salsa (the only one they sell)
4 (15 ounce) cans white beans, drained
1 cup half & half

Cook chicken and onion together; shred chicken and place in a large pot. Add the rest of the above ingredients except the beans and the half & half and simmer on low for about 30 minutes, stirring occasionally. Add drained beans and heat through about 10 minutes. Add half & half to chili before serving. Garnish with lime wedges, cilantro, shredded cheese, tortilla chips, sliced green onion.

    Adriana Molinaro   Granite Hills HS, El Cajon, CA

• •

Almond Cookies

Makes: 5 dozen cookies   ***China***

2 1/2 cups sifted flour
3/4 cup sugar
1 teaspoon baking powder
1/4 teaspoon salt
3/4 cup butter
1 egg
1 teaspoon almond extract
2 tablespoons water
72 blanched almonds

Preheat oven to 350 degrees. Sift together flour, sugar, baking powder and salt into bowl. Cut butter into flour mixture until it resembles coarse corn meal. Add egg, almond extract and water. Stir until mixture pulls away from the sides of the bowl. Knead on lightly floured board until smooth. Wrap and chill for an hour. Lightly grease 2 cookie sheets. Form dough into balls the size of walnuts and flatten to 1/4 inch thick. Place on cookie sheet and press almond into each cookie. Bake for 20 to 25 minutes. Cool.

"A fun and tasty addition to a Chinese meal."

Sharon Chavez   **Millikan HS, Long Beach, CA**

Asian Chicken and Noodles

Serves: 4   ***China***

1 package ramen noodles, chicken flavored
2 cups frozen stir fry vegetables
1 tablespoon vegetable oil
1 chicken breast, diced
1/4 cup stir fry sauce

In a large saucepan, bring to a boil 2 cups water. Add noodles and vegetables. Cook until water returns to a full rolling boil. Drain. Meanwhile, In a large saucepan, sauté diced chicken until brown. Add drained noodles and vegetables. Stir in seasoning packet from the ramen noodles and the 1/4 cup stir fry sauce. Heat for about a minute and serve.

"This is a fast and easy dish that kids really like."

LeeAnn Bitner   **Alta HS, Sandy, UT**

Asian Fried Bananas

Serves: 4-6   ***China***

2 large bananas
8 (7 inch square) spring roll wrappers
1 cup brown sugar, or to taste
1 quart oil for deep frying

Preheat the oil in a deep-fryer or large cast-iron skillet to 375 degrees F. Peel bananas, and slice them in half lengthwise, then crosswise into fourths. Place one piece of banana diagonally across the corner of a spring roll wrapper, and sprinkle with brown sugar to taste. Roll from the corner to the center, then fold top and bottom corners in, and continue rolling. Dip your finger in water and brush the last edge to seal. Repeat with remaining banana pieces. Fry a few banana rolls at a time in the hot oil until evenly browned. Remove to paper towels to drain. Serve hot or cold. Drizzle chocolate or caramel sauce. Can be served with ice cream.

"Great dessert, a little unexpected."

Linda Silvasy   Temecula MS, Temecula, CA

Asian Meatballs

Makes: 24   *China*

Meatballs:
1 pound ground beef
1 cup fine bread crumbs
1 egg
4 tablespoons green onion, finely chopped
1-2 cloves garlic, minced
1/4 cup catsup
Sauce:
1 cup pineapple juice
4 tablespoons soy sauce
2 teaspoons corn starch
3 tablespoons brown sugar
1/4 - 1/2 teaspoon fresh ginger, minced fine (optional but worth the trouble!)
Optional: a few drops of Sriracha (hot chili sauce)

Preheat oven to 375 degrees. Combine all the meatball ingredients and mix well. Shape into cocktail size meatballs, about 1 inch in diameter in size. You can use a small cookie scoop if you have one. Bake for 8 to 12 minutes. Mix all sauce ingredients together. Make sure all the cornstarch is dissolved before you put the pan on the heat. Stirring constantly, bring the mixture to a boil and then boil for one more minute. If desired, add chili sauce to taste. Add the meatballs to the sauce. Serve warm with party toothpicks. For an added garnish, you can slice fresh pineapple chunks and skewer them on the toothpicks to be enjoyed with the meatballs.

"This recipe is simple with a great Asian flavor. The fresh ginger really makes it special!"

Carissa McCrory   Whitney HS, Rocklin, CA

Beef Broccoli Stir Fry

Serves: 4-6   *China*

1 tablespoon cornstarch
2 tablespoons soy sauce
1 pound beef for stir fry
5 tablespoons oil
1/4 cup onion, chopped
1 clove garlic, minced
1/4 teaspoon crushed, dried red pepper
2 medium carrots, julienne strips
2 cups broccoli floweretts
1/2 cup beef broth

Mix cornstarch and soy sauce in a bowl. Add beef strips, stir to coat. Cover and refrigerate 4 hours or overnight. Drain, reserve marinade. In a large skillet or wok, heat 2 tablespoons oil over medium high heat. Add onion, garlic and red pepper. Stir fry for 2 minutes. Remove with slotted spoon to large bowl. Add 2 tablespoons oil. Add carrots and broccoli, stir fry for 2 minutes or until tender and crisp. Remove to bowl. Add 1 tablespoon oil, beef and stir fry 3 minutes or until lightly browned. Add beef broth and reserved marinade. Stir constantly, bring to a boil over medium heat for 1 minute. Add vegetables. Cook 2-3 minutes until heated. Serve over rice.

Suella Brown   **Sparks HS, Sparks, NV**

Chinese Fried Rice

Serves: 4   *China*

Cooked Rice:
1 cup rice
1 3/4 cups water
Chinese Fried Rice:
1 egg, beaten
1 tablespoon oil
1/2 cup diced pork, chicken, shrimp or any meat cooked in 1 tablespoon of oil
1-3 tablespoons oil
3 cups cold cooked rice
2 tablespoons soy sauce
1/2 teaspoon salt
1 cup frozen peas and carrots, cooked
1 green onion, chopped

Cooked Rice: Wash rice thoroughly in cold water several times until water is clear. Add water; bring to a boil. Reduce heat and cook 15 minutes. Cool rice completely; preferably refrigerate overnight on a sheet pan, separating rice into small clumps.
Chinese Fried Rice: Fry beaten egg like a tortilla in 1 tablespoon of oil and remove from wok. Cut into short thin strips. Cook raw meat in 1 tablespoon oil until cooked and remove from wok (optional). Add 1-3 tablespoons of oil followed by rice and stir-fry until thoroughly heated. Add the soy sauce by dribbling over the rice, mix well and then add salt. Add the cooked eggs, meat, peas,carrots and green onion.

Michele Casale   **San Mateo HS, San Mateo, CA**

Egg Rolls

Serves: 4   ***China***

1/2 pound hamburger, ground pork, chicken, or firm tofu
1 clove garlic, minced
1/2 teaspoon ginger, minced
1 cup cabbage, chopped
bean sprouts
1/2 cup carrots, shredded
1 green onion, chopped
1 tablespoon oyster sauce
10 large square egg roll wrappers (keep covered with a damp cloth)
oil for frying
catsup and mustard for dipping
sweet and sour sauce for dipping

Stir-fry meat or tofu, garlic and ginger in wok over medium-high heat until lightly browned, 2-3 minutes. Add cabbage, bean sprouts, carrots and green onion. Cook 2 minutes. Stir in oyster sauce. Let mixture cool a few minutes; stir once in a while to help cool. Use 2 tablespoons filling for each egg roll; don't overfill. Place filling diagonally on wrapper, fold corner over filling, tucking corner around filling. Roll snugly halfway, covering filling. Fold up both sides snugly against filling. Moisten edges of last corner and roll corner flap up to seal. Lay egg roll flap side down until ready to cook. Heat oil to 350 degrees in large skillet. Using tongs, put 2-3 egg rolls in at a time to cook. Turn occasionally; cook about 2-3 minutes or until golden brown. Drain on paper towels. Serve with dipping sauces.

"This is a recipe my students love. I got it from Kathy Ewing, a retired home economics teacher from Modesto. I use it time after time and everyone loves it."

Linda Johnson   **Enochs HS, Modesto, CA**

Fried Rice

Serves: 4-6   ***China***

2 cups long grain rice, cooked and chilled
1/2 pound Jimmy Dean light pork sausage
1/3 cup frozen mixed vegetables
2 green onions, chopped
1/2 cup mushrooms, chopped fine
1/4 cup water chestnuts, chopped
1-2 eggs, beaten and scrambled
2 tablespoons soy sauce

In a large skillet, fry sausage until no longer pink. Add cold rice, and stir to heat through. Add mixed vegetables, onions, water chestnuts and mushrooms. Stir until blended (do not over stir as the mixture will get mushy). Make a hole in the center of the mixture and add the beaten eggs. Cook the eggs first before blending it into the rice and vegetables. Stir in the soy sauce by sprinkling it carefully over the rice.

"This is an easy recipe in class. Before my demonstration, the students cook rice for 20 minutes which is the approximate time for the demonstration. They will refrigerate it over night and follow these directions the next day. A great way to use leftover rice."

Ruth Anne Mills   **Los Alisos IS, Mission Viejo, CA**

Fried Wontons with Sweet and Sour Sauce

Serves: 20 - 30   *China*

1/4 pound fresh ground pork
2 tablespoons water chestnuts, finely chopped
1 green onion, chopped
2 tablespoons beaten egg
1/4 teaspoon salt
dash pepper
1/2 package wonton skins

Combine pork, water chestnuts, green onion, egg, salt and pepper. Place wonton square on working surface. Place 1 teaspoon filling (no more) in the lower corner of wonton skin. Fold that corner over filling. Roll to tuck point under. Moisten two corner sides with water. Pull them together behind filled corner and overlap. Pour oil into wok or heavy skillet. Heat to 400 degrees. Add wontons a few at a time and cook about two minutes. Remove with slotted spoon and drain on paper towel. Serve with sweet and sour sauce.

"My advanced Foods classes love this recipe. Also a family favorite during the holidays."

Charlotte Runyan   Saddleback HS, Santa Ana, CA

Ham Fried Rice

Serves: 4   *China*

1/4 pound ham, cubed
1 tablespoon oil
1/2 cup celery, chopped small
1/4 cup carrots, grated
1 green onion, chopped
1 cup cooked rice
1 1/2 teaspoons soy sauce
1/4 teaspoon salt
1 egg

Sauté celery, carrots, and onion in oil until soft. Stir in rice, ham and seasonings. Beat egg with a fork then add to rice mixture. Cook until egg sets up.

"This is really good with chicken egg rolls."

LeeAnn Bitner   Alta HS, Sandy, UT

Holly's Gluten Free Stir Fry

Serves: 4 *China*

1/2 cup onion, chopped
1 cup celery slices
1 small clove garlic, minced
1 yellow squash, sliced
1 zucchini, sliced
1 red pepper, sliced
1 green pepper, sliced
1 orange pepper, sliced
1 yellow pepper, sliced
5 brussel sprouts, minced
1 cup carrots, thinly sliced
1 (14 ounces) can gluten free chicken broth
2 tablespoons gluten free soy sauce
1 cup fresh mushrooms, sliced
3 cups shredded cooked chicken
1 cup fresh pineapple chunks
1(5 ounce) can water chestnuts
3 tablespoons cornstarch
3 tablespoons water
1/2 cup gluten free sliced almonds

Using a wok or heavy frying pan, stir in the onion, celery, and garlic. Cook for 3 minutes. Add squash, zucchini, peppers, sprouts, and carrots. Cook another 3 minutes. Add the chicken broth and soy sauce. Heat to boiling. Add mushrooms, chicken, pineapple, and water chestnuts. Cover and simmer for 5 minutes. Do not overcook. Mix the cornstarch and water in a separate bowl. Stir into chicken mixture and cook until the liquid thickens, 1 or 2 minutes. Taste and add salt if necessary (this depends on the saltiness of the broth). Pour the stir-fry onto a serving platter and top with almonds. Serve rice separately.

"My daughter, Holly, was able to adapt this stir-fry recipe to her gluten free diet with minor changes. You can't even tell the difference!"

Rhonda Nelson   RSM IS, Rancho Santa Margarita, CA

Honey Orange Chicken

Serves: 4 *China*

3 chicken breasts, cubed
1/2 cup honey
2 tablespoons vinegar
1/2 cup orange juice
2 tablespoons soy sauce
2 teaspoons cornstarch
2 tablespoons cooking oil

Cube chicken into one-inch chunks and set aside. For the sauce, stir together honey, vinegar, orange juice, soy sauce, and cornstarch in a small bowl and set aside. Pour oil into large skillet and heat to medium-high. Add chicken, cooking until no longer pink. Push chicken from the center of the skillet to the side of the pan. Stir sauce one more

Chinese Pork Dumplings

Makes: 4 dozen or 16 servings (3 per serving)   **China**

8 ounces Ground Pork
1/4 cup Chinese sausage, finely chopped (Find this at your local
   Chinese Grocery or substitute it with 1/4 cup finely chopped
   pieces of cooked ham and 1/2 teaspoon of brown sugar).
1/4 cup carrot, shredded
1 1/2 teaspoons scallions, minced
1 1/2 teaspoons garlic, minced (3 cloves)
1 1/2 teaspoons Chinese seasoned rice wine
1 1/2 teaspoons soy sauce
1 1/2 teaspoons Oriental sesame oil
1 teaspoon ginger, minced
1/4 teaspoon salt
1/8 teaspoon white pepper
Napa cabbage leaves, to line the steamer basket
Chinese Golden Egg Pasta Dumpling Wrappers:
3 cups flour
1 tablespoon turmeric
1 egg
2 tablespoons peanut oil
1 cup water, warm

For filling, combine the pork, sausage, carrot, scallions, garlic, rice wine, soy sauce, sesame oil, ginger, salt and pepper in large bowl, and mix thoroughly so that...

(Continued on page 144)

Gingered Pork Vegetable Soup with Wonton Noodles

Serves: 4   **China**

1 cooked pork tenderloin, cut into 1/2-inch cubes
3 cups chicken broth, reduced-sodium
1 1/2 cups water
1/4 cup rice wine vinegar
1 tablespoon soy sauce, reduced-sodium
2 cloves garlic, minced (1 teaspoon)
1 teaspoon ginger, grated
1/4 teaspoon black pepper
8 whole baby corn, canned, quartered crosswise
2 ounces fresh snow peas, halved crosswise
1/2 cup carrot, thinly bias-sliced
1/2 cup sliced mushrooms
1/4 cup green onions, or chives thinly sliced
8 3 1/2-inch wonton wrappers, cut into 1/2-inch-wide strip

Combine chicken broth, water, rice wine vinegar, soy sauce, garlic, gingerroot and black pepper in large saucepan. Bring to boil. Separate the wonton strips. Stir in corn, snow peas, carrot, mushrooms, onions and wonton strips. Return to a boil; reduce heat. Cover and simmer about 3 minutes or until vegetables are crisp-tender. Stir in pork and heat through.

National Pork Board   PorkBeInspired.com

Chinese Pork Dumplings

Gingered Pork Vegetable Soup With Wonton Noodles

Asparagus Frittata with
Red Bell Peppers

Mediterranean Kiwi
Couscous

Asparagus Frittata with Red Bell Peppers

Serves: 6   *Italy*

1 lb. California asparagus, trimmed
   and blanched
salt, as needed
1 red bell pepper, julienned
1/2 cup onion, chopped
2 tablespoons olive oil
8 eggs, beaten
2 tablespoons Italian parsley, chopped

1/4 teaspoon salt
¼ teaspoon freshly ground pepper
4 oz. Feta cheese, crumbled
   (about 1 cup)
1-1/2 tablespoon butter, softened
lemon wedges
sprigs of Italian parsley for garnish

Reserve 6 asparagus spears. Cut remaining asparagus at an angle into 1-inch pieces, reserve. Sauté bell pepper in 2 tablespoons olive oil until soft, but not browned, about 7 minutes. Stir in onion and reserved asparagus pieces; sauté for 1 minute. With a slotted spoon remove vegetables to drain on paper toweling, reserve. Whisk chopped parsley, salt and pepper into beaten eggs. Stir in cheese and reserved sautéed vegetables. Coat the inside of a heavy, non-stick 12-inch frying pan (with a cover) with softened butter. Pour egg mixture into pan. Bake in a preheated 350 degree oven, covered, until eggs are just firm, about 35 minutes. Remove cover; bake until top is lightly browned, about 10 minutes. Loosen the frittata, then cover pan with a large, warmed serving platter. Flip frying pan over onto platter. Cut frittata into 6 wedges; garnish each with 1 reserved asparagus spear. Divide wedges among 6 serving plates, then put a lemon wedge and a sprig of parsley on each plate. Use a cheese planer or a potato peeler to shave cheese paper thin.

California Asparagus Commission

Mediterranean Kiwi Couscous

Serves: 4 to 6   *Greece*

3/4 cup water
1/2 cup couscous
salt
3 California kiwifruit
1 yellow or orange pepper
1 cup colourful cherry tomatoes
1/4 cup Kalamata olives,
   preferably spicy

3 green onions, thinly sliced
1 tbsp red wine vinegar
3 tbsp olive oil
1 garlic clove, minced
1 tsp dried oregano leaves
pepper
1/2 cup crumbled feta cheese
1/2 cup shredded fresh basil

In a small saucepan, lightly salt water then bring to a boil. Add couscous, stir, cover and remove from heat. Let stand until water is absorbed, about 5 minutes. Meanwhile, peel kiwifruit and cut into bite-size chunks. Dice pepper and slice large cherry tomatoes in half. Pit olives if needed and thinly slice green onions. Place all in a medium bowl. Whisk vinegar with oil, garlic, oregano and generous pinches salt and pepper. When couscous has cooled, gently stir with kiwifruit mixture. Toss with as much dressing as needed to just coat. Stir in feta and basil. Salad will keep well refrigerated for 1 to 2 days.

California Kiwifruit Commission

time in the bowl then add to center of the skillet. Cook and stir sauce until thickened and bubbly. Mix in the chicken to thoroughly coat. Serve over rice.

"My class makes this every year during our international foods unit and it is always a hit. This is a lighter, healthier version than you would get at a fast food Chinese restaurant."

Shasta Jolly   Villa Park HS, Villa Park, CA

Hot and Sour Tofu Soup

Serves: 6   *China*

        8 dried shiitake mushrooms
        1 tablespoon vegetable oil
        1 garlic clove, minced
        1 tablespoon fresh ginger, finely minced
        6 cups vegetable or chicken broth
        1 pound firm tofu, drained, cut into 1/2-inch cubes
        1/4 cup rice vinegar
        2 tablespoons soy sauce
        1/4 cup cornstarch
        1/2 teaspoon white pepper
        1/4 teaspoon hot chili oil
        4 green onions, white and green parts thinly sliced
        1 cup Chinese chow mien noodles

Soak mushrooms in very hot water for 30 minutes. Drain. Squeeze dry. Remove tough stems. Cut caps in thin strips and set aside. In a frying pan, heat oil over medium heat and sauté garlic and ginger briefly. In a stock pot, bring broth to a boil and add the sliced mushrooms. Add the tofu, cover and simmer until hot. In a bowl, blend together the rice vinegar, soy sauce and cornstarch until smooth. Stir into soup. Cook, stirring, until soup boils. Add the white pepper and chili oil. Simmer a few minutes. Ladle into bowls. Top with green onions. Offer Chinese chow mein noodles when served.

"I have been making this soup for many years at home. Last year my Catering students prepared it for a multi-cultural luncheon. It received many, many rave reviews!"

Margo Olsen   Amador Valley and Foothill HS, Pleasanton, CA

Kung Pao Chicken

Serves: 4-6   *China*

1 chicken breast, boned, skinned and cut into cubes
water chestnuts, cut in fourths
bamboo shoots
1 zucchini, chopped
1/2 bell pepper, diced (red and green)
1 green onion, cut in 1/4 inch pieces
2 cloves garlic, minced
4 tablespoons oil
1/4 cup chicken stock
2 tablespoons roasted peanuts
Marinade:
2 teaspoons soy sauce
1 teaspoon mirin
1 teaspoon cornstarch
1 tablespoon vegetable oil
Seasonings:
2 teaspoons soy sauce
1 teaspoon mirin
1 teaspoon rice vinegar
2 teaspoons sugar
1 teaspoon corn starch
1/2 teaspoon salt
dried red chili pods or pinch red chili flakes

Cut chicken into 3/4 inch cubes. Combine with marinade and set aside. Add 2 tablespoons oil to wok and set to high. Heat for 1 minute. Add chicken, stirring to separate pieces; remove. Combine seasonings and set aside. Add 2 tablespoons oil and chili pods to wok. Heat. Sauté garlic. Return chicken to wok. Add vegetables and seasonings. Deglaze with chicken stock. Cook until thickened. Garnish with peanuts.

Michele Casale   **San Mateo HS, San Mateo, CA**

Luscious Turkey Lo Mein

Serves: 6   *China*

8 ounces lo mein or udon noodles or spaghetti, uncooked
2 tablespoons vegetable oil, divided
1 package Jennie-O Turkey Store Turkey Breast cutlets, cut into 3/4 inch chunks
2 teaspoons minced ginger, bottled or fresh
2 teaspoons minced garlic, bottled or fresh
1/4 teaspoon crushed red pepper flakes
2 cups bok choy, sliced or fresh sugar snap peas
1 cup thin red bell pepper strips
1/4 cup chicken broth
1/4 cup soy sauce or tamari
2 tablespoons oyster sauce
2 tablespoons dark sesame oil

Cook noodles according to package directions. Meanwhile, heat 1 tablespoon oil in a large deep skillet over medium-high heat. Add turkey, ginger, garlic and pepper flakes; stir-fry 3 minutes. Transfer to a bowl; set aside. Add remaining 1 tablespoon oil to skillet. Add bok choy and bell pepper; stir-fry 2 minutes. Add broth, soy sauce, and oyster sauce; bring to a simmer. Add turkey and sesame oil to skillet; simmer 2

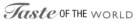

minutes or until turkey is no longer pink in center. Drain noodles; add to skillet and heat through. Serve in shallow soup bowls.

"This Jennie-O Turkey Store recipe is great to use to teach the stir-fry technique, as well as to give students a way to use the many fresh turkey products available at the grocery store. It is also great prepared with ground turkey."

Leigh Ann Diffenderfer   **Newbury Park HS, Newbury Park, CA**

Orange Flavored Chicken
Serves: 4   *China*

Sauce:
1 1/2 cups water
2 tablespoons orange juice
1 cup dark brown sugar, packed
1/3 cup rice vinegar
2 1/2 tablespoons soy sauce
1/4 cup plus 1 teaspoon lemon juice
1 teaspoon water chestnuts, minced
1/2 teaspoon fresh ginger, minced
1 teaspoon green onion, chopped
1/4 teaspoon garlic, minced
1/4 teaspoon crushed red pepper flakes
5 teaspoons corn starch
2 teaspoons arrowroot
Chicken:
4 breast fillets
1 cup ice water
1 egg
1/4 teaspoon baking soda
1/4 teaspoon salt
1 1/2 cups unsifted cake flour
2 to 4 cups vegetable oil

Combine sauce ingredients, except corn starch and arrowroot, in small saucepan over high heat. Bring to boil, stirring often. Remove from heat and cool, uncovered. Slice chicken into bite-size chunks. Pour 1 cup sauce over chicken and marinate in plastic bag for 2 to 3 hours. Heat 2 inches of oil in wok or skillet to 350 degrees. Combine corn starch and arrowroot, add 3 tablespoons water. Stir until dissolved. Stir into sauce and heat until it bubbles. Cover and remove from heat. Beat egg and ice water. Add soda and salt. Add 3/4 cups flour and stir with fork until blended. Sprinkle 1/4 cups flour on top of batter and mix with one or two strokes only. (Most of new flour will float on top.) Dip chicken into flour, then batter. Fry 3 to 4 minutes or until golden brown. Flip chicken over halfway through the cooking time. Remove and drain. Reheat covered sauce and stir. When chicken is cooked, put in large bowl and cover with thickened sauce. Stir gently.

"Just like the Orange Chicken everyone loves."

Donna Baker   **Redlands East Valley HS, Redlands, CA**

Sesame Noodles

Serves: 2-4

9 ounces spaghetti pasta
3 tablespoons soy sauce
2 teaspoons sugar
2 large cloves garlic, minced
1 1/2 tablespoons rice vinegar
1 1/2 tablespoons pure sesame oil
2 tablespoons plus 1 teaspoon canola oil
3 tablespoons Sweetened Chili Sauce
1 1/2 tablespoons hot water
2 1/2 green onions, sliced thin (green part only)
4 slices (or more) bacon, cooked and cut into small pieces
    or 1/2 - 1 cup chicken, shredded and then diced

Prepare pasta per instructions. Keep warm in pot after draining. Whisk together the soy sauce, sugar, garlic, vinegar, oils, chili sauce and water in a small bowl. Taste and re-season if necessary. Mix the sauce with the pasta, tossing well. Add in the green onion and the bacon and/or chicken and serve hot.

"Easy recipe that the kids love. You can adjust the seasonings to your liking!"

Beckie Bloemker   **Foothill HS, Sacramento, CA**

Sweet and Sour Chicken

Serves: 4

4 boneless, skinless chicken breasts, cut into chunks
cornstarch, to coat chicken pieces
pineapple, cut in chunks
onion, cut in chunks
green pepper, cut in chunks
Sweet and Sour Sauce:
1 1/2 cups sugar
1 cup cider vinegar
1/2 cup ketchup
1/2 cup chicken bouillon
2 tablespoons soy sauce

Coat chicken pieces with cornstarch. Fry in small amount of oil. Combine ingredients for sweet and sour sauce in separate pan; bring to a boil. Add sauce to chicken pieces along with pineapple, onion and green pepper. Simmer for 30 to 45 minutes or until sauce thickens. Serve over rice.

"Can also be made with pork or shrimp. Also good served with Vegetable Lo Mein."

Shelly Tresley   **Cold Springs MS, Reno, NV**

Sweet and Sour Sauce
Makes: about 2 cups   *China*

1/3 cup rice vinegar
1 cup water
3/4 cup granulated sugar
1/2 teaspoon salt
pinch white pepper
4 drops Tabasco sauce
2 tablespoons corn starch
2 tablespoons cold water
3 tablespoons ketchup
1/2 teaspoon fresh minced ginger

In a small sauce pan, over medium heat, bring vinegar, water, sugar, salt, pepper and Tabasco to a boil, stir to dissolve sugar. In a small bowl, combine corn starch and cold water. Add the corn starch slurry to the boiling mixture and cook, stirring constantly until thick and bubbly. Remove from heat, add ketchup and ginger.

"Quick and Delicious. Better than the sauce from the restaurant."

Shauna Young   **Jordan HS, Sandy, UT**

Sweet and Sour Spareribs
Serves: 6   *China*

3 pounds spareribs, cut into bite-sized pieces
1 clove garlic, minced
1/4 teaspoon ginger, grated
1 teaspoon salt
1/4 teaspoon black pepper
3 tablespoons sugar
3/4 cup vinegar
2 tablespoons soy sauce
1/2 cup catsup

Preheat oven to 325 degrees. Place ribs in a baking pan. Bake for 1 hour. Drain fat. In a small bowl, combine garlic, ginger, salt, black pepper, sugar, vinegar, soy sauce and catsup. Pour sauce over ribs then bake an additional 45 minutes until ribs are done.

"A family favorite from grandma's kitchen."

Reiko Ikkanda   **South Pasadena MS, South Pasadena, CA**

Szechwan-Style Chicken
Serves: 6   *China*

2 boneless chicken breasts
1/3 cup teriyaki sauce
3 tablespoons Szechwan spicy stir-fry sauce
2 teaspoons cornstarch
1 tablespoon oil
1 large onion, chopped (1 cup)
3 cups bok choy, chopped
1 cup broccoli floweretts
1 medium red sweet pepper, cut into strips
2 carrots, chopped (1 cup)
2 zucchini, chopped (1 cup)

Rinse chicken and pat dry. Cut into thin strips. Set aside. Mix the sauce in a separate bowl. Mix together teriyaki sauce, Szechwan sauce, and cornstarch, set aside. Cut all vegetables before beginning to cook. Add 1 tablespoon oil to the wok. (Add more oil as necessary during cooking.) Preheat over medium-high heat. Stir-fry onion in hot oil for 2 minutes. Add bok choy, broccoli, red pepper, carrots, and zucchini. Stir-fry for 1 minute. Add the bok choy leaves; stir-fry 1 to 2 minutes more or until the vegetables are crisp tender. Remove vegetables from the pan. Set aside. Add 2 tablespoons oil to the wok. Add the chicken to the hot wok. Stir-fry for 2 to 3 minutes or until no pink remains. Add the vegetables back to the wok. Make a well in the center of the wok. Stir sauce. Add sauce to the center of the wok. Cook and stir until thickened and bubbly. Stir all ingredients together to coat with sauce. Cook and stir about 1 minute. Serve immediately over hot cooked rice.

"This recipe is hot and spicy. Add less Szechwan sauce if you don't like it hot! This recipe is a class favorite! Enjoy."

Pat Freshour   Foothill HS, Palo Cedro, CA

Vegetable Chow Mein

Serves: 4   *China*

8 ounces fresh or dried chow mein noodles
3 tablespoons oil
3 cloves garlic
1 inch fresh ginger, peeled and minced
2 cups broccoli florets
2 carrots, chopped or slivered
2 cups bell peppers, diced or slivered
1 cup mushrooms
1/2 cup water chestnuts
1 cup Tofu, cut into small cubes
1/4 cup low sodium chicken broth
2 tablespoons hoisen sauce
2 tablespoons soy sauce
2 tablespoons honey
salt and pepper, to taste

Boil noodles in a large pot of water until tender, drain and pat dry. Heat oil in wok or large skillet, sauté garlic and ginger until lightly browned, then add cooked noodles and sauté until lightly browned. Add chopped vegetables and sauté for about three minutes. Add Tofu. Add chicken broth, hoisen, soy sauce, and honey. Bring to a boil, and cook until mixture is reduced and slightly thickened. Season with salt and pepper to taste.

"This is a Giada DeLauentis recipe that I altered to make it more "lab friendly." The students loved it - a great way to introduce tofu to students who have never tried it."

Cyndi Murdoch   Orland HS, Orland, CA

Vegetable Lo Mein

Serves: 8   *China*

3/4 pound spaghetti
2 tablespoons oil, divided
5 quarter size slices (1/4 in thick) fresh unpeeled ginger, minced
3 cloves garlic, minced
1/4 cup cilantro sprigs, packed
4 scallions, chopped
1/4 pound bean sprouts
1 large red bell pepper, sliced
1/2 small head cabbage, shredded
1/4 pound fresh spinach
1 package mushrooms, sliced
2/3 cup chicken broth
1/4 cup soy sauce
1 tablespoon cornstarch
1 tablespoon sherry
3 drops hot pepper sauce
1/4 teaspoon red pepper flakes
1/4 teaspoon pepper

Cook spaghetti and drain. Mince garlic and ginger. Chop scallions and bell pepper. Shred cabbage. Heat 1 tablespoon oil over medium high heat. Add ginger, garlic and cilantro. Stir fry about 2 min. Add 1 tablespoon oil and all vegetables, cook 4 minutes. In small bowl, combine chicken broth, soy sauce, cornstarch, sherry, hot pepper sauce, red and black pepper. Add pasta to vegetable mixture with broth mixture. Bring to boil. Cook about 2 minutes more.

"Sauce can easily be doubled or tripled. Can also add cooked chicken or pork."
Shelly Tresley   **Cold Springs MS, Reno, NV**

Indonesian Peanut Chicken

Serves: 4   *Indonesia*

3 chicken breasts, boneless, skinless, cut into 1 inch cubes
Marinade:
1/2 cup chunky peanut butter
1/2 cup peanut oil
1/4 cup white wine vinegar
1/4 cup soy sauce
1/4 cup fresh lemon juice
4 cloves garlic
8 cilantro sprigs
1/2 teaspoon crushed red pepper flakes
2 teaspoons fresh ginger, finely chopped

Marinade: Combine all ingredients in a blender. Cover and blend until smooth. Add a few drops of water if too thick. Reserve about 1 cup of marinade for dipping sauce. Place remaining marinade in bowl. Add chicken and mix to coat. Marinate 2 to 3 hours in the refrigerator, stirring several times. Remove from refrigerator about 30 minutes before grilling. Preheat grill. Soak wooden skewers in water for 20 minutes. Thread 4 to 5 pieces of chicken on each skewer. Grill over medium-high coals for 8 to 10 minutes, turning often. Pass reserved marinade for dipping.

"One of our summer favorites on the barbecue. Serve with cilantro rice and fruit salad."

Kris Hawkins   Clovis West HS, Clovis, CA

Kue Lapis

Makes: 2 8" round cakes   *Indonesia*

  3 (13.5 ounce) cans coconut milk
  2 1/2 cups granulated sugar
  3 cups tapioca flour
  1 cup rice flour
  dash of salt
  1 teaspoon Pandan Flavoring
  red food coloring

Mix above ingredients together until smooth. Divide batter evenly between two bowls. In one bowl, add enough red food coloring to make a nice red batter. Leave the other bowl white. In a greased, round 8-inch aluminum cake pan, pour about 2 cups of the red batter and steam for 15 minutes. Pour 2 cups white batter over the steamed red batter and steam for 15 minutes. Alternate colors and steam 15 minutes each time until all batter is used up. Make sure you allow for 2 round cakes. Let cakes sit on counter till very cool, the Lapis will firm up. Do not cut until very firm and cut into thin wedges. Best to use a plastic knife to cut.

"It is fun to peel each layer off as you eat it."

Astrid Curfman   Newcomb Academy, Long Beach, CA

Asian Lettuce Wrap

Serves: 4   *Japan*

  1 tablespoon peanut oil
  1 bunch scallions, sliced (use entire scallion)
  1-2 cloves garlic, minced
  1 pound ground turkey or chicken, browned (dark meat preferable)
  Binder Sauce:
  1 tablespoon chicken bouillon
  1 tablespoon sugar
  1 teaspoon cornstarch
  1 tablespoon oyster sauce
  3 tablespoons soy sauce
  2 teaspoons ginger, freshly grated
  1 (8 ounce) can water chestnuts, small dice
  1 1/2 cups cabbage, shredded
  1/2 cup carrots, shredded
  green leaf lettuce

Sauté scallions & garlic in peanut oil. Add cooked turkey or chicken, heat through. In a separate bowl, combine chicken bouillon, sugar, cornstarch, oyster sauce, soy sauce, and grated ginger. Add to meat and heat thoroughly. Add water chestnuts. Turn off heat and add cabbage and carrots. Let cool before wrapping in lettuce leaves.

"Healthy and easy to make."

Peggy Herndon   Central Valley HS, Shasta Lake, CA

California Rolls

Makes: 2 rolls   *Japan*

1 avocado
1/2 cucumber
1 to 3 carrots, peeled
3 cups short grain rice
1/4 cup crab meat or imitation crab
2 tablespoons mayonnaise
2 sheets seaweed wrap

Slice the avocado, cucumber and carrots into thin slices. Prepare rice according to package directions or in rice cooker. Mix crab meat with mayonnaise. Place seaweed wrap on a flat surface. Spread sticky rice all across seaweed wrap. Place carrots, avocado and cucumber on top of the rice parallel to each other. Spread meat on top; roll. Slice into sections.

"Born and raised Californian. I thought this recipe would be fitting for a Cali girl. A student made this as a demonstration in our foods class."

Julie Eyre   **Alhambra HS, Alhambra, CA**

Green Rolls

Makes: 16 pieces   *Japan*

1 head of Napa cabbage (regular green is ok too), peel leaves apart from core
1 bunch collard greens
1/2 head purple cabbage, peel leaves apart from core
A variety of vegetables can be substituted, taking care to boil the
  more colorful or bitter vegetables separately or last.
Sauce:
2 tablespoons toasted sesame oil
1/4 cup spring or filtered water
1/4 cup soy sauce
1-2 tablespoons toasted sesame seeds
2 tablespoons mirin (Japanese cooking wine)

Wash each vegetable. Boil a large pot of water. Blanche the Napa cabbage leaves by adding them to the water for 30-60 seconds (summertime needs less cooking time). Remove and lay them out to cool. Repeat the process with the collard greens, then the purple cabbage. Lay out one Napa cabbage leaf with outside facing down. Layer the collard, followed by the purple cabbage on top. Roll the layers up together so they make a tight roll. Squeeze gently to drain off the excess water. The process can also be done on a sushi mat. With a sharp knife, slice into 1 1/2" pieces. Turn up on their sides to serve. *Sauce:* Add all ingredients to a saucepan and heat until warm but not boiling. Serve on side as dipping sauce.

"This is from a class I taught called, "Cooking for Natural Beauty". This recipe makes me feel very relaxed and refreshed. My family was very impressed when I made a batch for a holiday dinner too because they look good and taste delicious."

Kim Allen   **Temple City HS, Temple City, CA**

Oriental Fried Chicken

Serves: 5-6   *Japan*

Marinade:
4 tablespoons flour
8 tablespoons cornstarch
4 tablespoons sugar
1 1/2 teaspoons salt
3 tablespoons soy sauce
2 eggs
2 tablespoons green onions, chopped
1 clove garlic, minced
3 1/2 pounds chicken drumettes

In a large bowl, combine all the ingredients for the marinade. Add chicken drumettes to the marinade then soak for at least 2 hours or overnight. Fry drumettes in 3/4 inch oil in frying pan over medium/high heat. Can be served warm or cold.

"Great for parties and picnics."

Reiko Ikkanda   South Pasadena MS, South Pasadena, CA

Yakitori (Chicken Skewers)

Makes: 4   *Japan*

4-6 chicken thighs
8 green onions
1/2 cup soy sauce
1/4 cup Mirin or sake
1/4 cup sugar
2 tablespoons honey
24 small wooden spears, soaked in cool water for at least one hour

Mix together soy sauce, sugar, honey, mirin, and heat it up until it's homogenous. You can heat it in the microwave or in a saucepan. Chill. Cut thigh meat off bone leaving muscle in one piece. Cut into 1 x 4 x 6 inch pieces. Soak in chilled marinade several hours or overnight. Cut green onion in half lengthwise. Lay the green onion and chicken on top of each other and thread the wooden skewer through both. Broil or grill until chicken is done! Watch them. they burn fast!

"This is a popular lunch and snack item in Japan."

Priscilla Burns   Pleasant Valley HS, Chico, CA

Bulgogi (Korean Fire Meat)

Serves: 6   *Korea*

2 pounds lean beef
4 tablespoons sugar
1/2 cup soy sauce
1/4 cup sesame oil
2 tablespoons sesame seeds
2 green onions, chopped
1 1/2 teaspoons garlic powder
1 teaspoon pepper

43

Cut beef across grain into thin strips. Combine remaining ingredients for marinade and pour over meat in bowl. Cover, let marinate for 4-24 hours. Cook in wok until meat is done (about 5 minutes). Serve over rice.

"Students love this."

Janet Hough

Foothill HS, Henderson, NV

Korean Barbecued Short Ribs

Serves: 4

Korea

4 pounds meaty beef short ribs
1/2 cup soy sauce
1 tablespoon cider vinegar
2 green onions minced
2 cloves garlic, minced
1 tablespoon finely minced ginger root
3 tablespoons sugar
1/4 cup sesame oil
1 teaspoon dried red pepper flakes
1/4 cup sesame seeds
1 tablespoon flour

Make deep cuts in the meat between the ribs so the meat will absorb the marinade. Rub well with sugar and oil and let sit for 30 minutes. Combine ingredients, pour over ribs, and let stand for 1 hour. Bake or barbecue, turning and basting frequently with marinade, for 20 to 30 minutes or until meat is cooked.

"Everyone loves this recipe, the ribs fall off the bone and are really tasty!"

Tracy Shannon

Swope MS, Reno, Nevada

Lumpia

Makes: 2 dozen

Philippines

1/2 pound ground beef
2 garlic cloves, finely chopped
1/2 large brown onion, finely chopped
1/2 small head of cabbage, thinly shredded
3 large carrots, finely grated
1/4 pound bean sprouts
Accent, to taste
salt and white pepper, to taste
package egg roll wrappers
oil for frying

In large skillet, brown ground beef. Add garlic, onion, cabbage, carrots, and bean sprouts. Fry until vegetables have softened. Add accent, pepper and salt, to taste. Drain liquid and allow to cool. Place about one heaping tablespoon of filling in bottom eighth of wrapper. Fold over, covering filling. Fold both sides in. Roll rest up into the wrapper. Heat oil to 375 degrees. Fry lumpia until golden brown.

"I grew up with this appetizer and we always had it when there was a get-together."

Astrid Curfman

Newcomb Academy, Long Beach, CA

Jeff's Grilled Ahi Tuna & Thai BBQ Sauce

Serves: 4   *Thailand*

1/2 cup bottled BBQ sauce
2 tablespoons 3 Crabs Fish Sauce
1-3 tablespoons Sriracha Chili Sauce, to taste
2 teaspoons soy sauce
1 teaspoon garlic, chopped
4 Ahi Tuna Steaks, 1 1/2 inch thick

Combine the first five ingredients to make the sauce. Make the sauce one day ahead if possible. Defrost tuna with great care to prevent histamine poisoning. Defrost on the top shelf of the refrigerator over a day or two. It is a good idea to take the fish out of the refrigerator about an hour before grilling so the center isn't super cold. The cook times will be accurate to achieve a rare center. Sear fish on a very hot grill for approximately 1 and 1/2 minutes per side. Brush with sauce as it comes off the grill. Serve.

"This recipe is my husband's original creation. He is an avid fisherman so we usually have an abundance of fresh fish."

Delaine Smith   West Valley HS, Cottonwood, CA

Thai Chicken Pasta

Serves: 4   *Thailand*

3 cloves garlic, minced
1/4 cup soy sauce
1 tablespoon sesame oil
2 teaspoons crushed red pepper
1 teaspoon cumin
1 teaspoon ground ginger
1/4 cup creamy peanut butter
3 tablespoons canola oil
1 pound spaghetti
1 pound chicken breast, sliced into narrow strips
1 tablespoon peanut oil
1 jalapeno pepper, diced (optional)
5 green onions, sliced
1/2 cup cilantro
1/2 cup shredded carrots
1/2 cup bean sprouts
1/4 cup peanuts, chopped (optional)

Make the Sauce. Combine the garlic, soy sauce, sesame oil, red pepper, cumin, ginger, peanut butter, and canola oil in a small bowl and whisk until all of the ingredients are combined and smooth. Set aside. Cook the pasta according to the directions on the package. Stir-fry the chicken breast in the peanut oil for 5-7 minutes. Add the jalapeno pepper if desired, then add the green onion, and stir for 3 minutes more. Place the chicken in a large serving bowl. Add the cooked, drained pasta to the bowl with the chicken and toss with the sauce, cilantro, carrots and sprouts. Serve. Note: This can be served at room temperature or chilled.

"My husband likes this to have more sauce so I have to double the sauce recipe."

Betty Rabin-Fung   Retired Sierra Vista JHS, Canyon Country, CA

Thai Lettuce Wraps

Serves: 4   *Thailand*

1 pound ground beef
1 clove garlic, minced
1/2 red onion, finely chopped
1 teaspoon chili paste
1/2 teaspoon red pepper flakes
1/2 teaspoon rice wine vinegar
1 tablespoon soy sauce
3 cups cooked rice
1 head of leaf lettuce or iceburg lettuce, leaves separated
1 carrot, thinly sliced with vegetable peeler

Cook rice. Brown meat in skillet. Drain fat. Add garlic, onion, chili paste, red pepper and soy sauce. Cook for 3 to 4 minutes to blend flavors. Serve meat mixture, peeled carrots, rice and lettuce on separate plates to allow guest to assemble themselves. Wrap like a burrito/egg roll in lettuce leaves.

Janet Hough   **Foothill HS, Henderson, NV**

Thai Mango Rice

Serves: 4-6   *Thailand*

2 mangoes, peeled
2 cups coconut milk
4 tablespoons sugar
4 pinches salt
2 cups cooked sticky rice

Puree the peeled mangoes. Scald the coconut milk and add the sugar and salt. Mix the sticky rice together with 1 1/2 cups of the coconut milk. Let stand five minutes. Divide rice mixture into serving bowls and pour the mango puree over the top. Pour the other 1/2 cup of coconut milk over the top of the mango puree.

"This authentic recipe came from one of my Thai students."

Peggy Herndon   **Central Valley HS, Shasta Lake, CA**

Thai Sweet Potato Coconut Red Curry

Serves: 6   *Thailand*

2 pounds sweet potatoes
2 (13.5 ounce) cans coconut milk
red curry paste, to taste
2 tablespoons fish sauce
1 tablespoon palm or brown sugar
1/2 cup torn basil leaves
brown rice, cooked

Peel and cut sweet potatoes into 1 inch cubes and place in a large pot. Add coconut milk, curry paste, fish sauce and sugar. Cover and cook until sweet potato is tender. Stir in basil leaves right before serving. Serve over brown rice.

"Sometimes it is hard to find recipes for sweet potatoes. This is a good one if you like spicy Thai food. You can add more basil, onions or other veggies if you want but you may have to add more coconut milk if you do so."

Janet Tingley   **Atascadero HS, Atascadero, CA**

Australia

●●●

Pavlova
Serves: 8   *Australia*

   6 egg whites
   1/4 teaspoon salt
   1 2/3 cups sugar
   1 tablespoon cornstarch
   1 teaspoon white vinegar
   1 teaspoon vanilla
   whipping cream
   assorted berries for topping

Preheat oven to 325 degrees. Line a cookie sheet with parchment. Beat egg whites with salt in electric mixer on high until soft peaks form. Begin adding sugar a little at a time until all is incorporated. Continue to mix until egg whites form stiff, glossy peaks. Gently fold in cornstarch, vinegar and vanilla. Spread mixture onto parchment in a circle about 8 inches across and 2 inches tall. Bake for 30 minutes and reduce temperature to 280 degrees and bake further for 40 minutes. Turn oven off and prop door open an inch. Allow pavlova to cool in the oven. Top with whipped cream and berries to serve.

   "Our family was introduced to this recipe by Eliza, our Australian exchange student. We now make this for every special occasion to share our memories of Eliza's visit."

   Debbie Harvey   **Amador Valley HS, Pleasanton, CA**

Bananas Brazilian Style

Serves: 6   ***Brazil***

  6 medium bananas
  1/2 cup orange juice
  1 tablespoon fresh lemon juice
  1/4 cup brown sugar
  2 tablespoons butter
  1 cup coconut, fresh grated

Preheat oven to 400 degrees. Peel the bananas and cut them lengthwise. Place in a buttered baking dish. Combine the orange juice, lemon juice, and brown sugar and pour it over the bananas. Dot with butter. Bake for 10 to 15 minutes. Sprinkle with the grated coconut.

  Val Logie   **Ladera Ranch MS, Ladera Ranch, CA**

Brazilian Candies (Brigadeiros)

Serves: 20   ***Brazil***

  3 tablespoons unsweetened cocoa
  1 tablespoon margarine
  1 can sweetened condensed milk

In a medium saucepan, combine the ingredients and cook over medium heat, stirring until thickened, about 15 minutes. Remove from heat and chill until cool enough to roll into small balls. Roll in more cocoa or chocolate sprinkles. Enjoy!

  Patty Bulat   **Rogers MS, Long Beach, CA**

Black Bean Burgers

Serves: 4-6   ***Central America***

  2 (14 ounce) cans black beans, rinsed & drained, divided
  3 tablespoons mayonnaise
  1/3 cup plain dry bread crumbs
  2 teaspoons ground cumin
  1 teaspoon dried oregano, crumbled
  1/4 teaspoon cayenne
  1/4 cup cilantro, finely chopped
  3 tablespoons vegetable oil
  4-6 hamburger buns

Add 1 can beans, mayonnaise, bread crumbs and spices to work bowl of food processor. Pulse mixture until a coarse puree forms. Transfer mixture to bowl; stir in cilantro and remaining can of whole beans. Form mixture into 4-6 patties. Heat oil in heavy skillet over med-high heat until it shimmers. Cook patties until outsides are crisp and lightly browned, turning once, about 5 minutes total. Serve on hamburger buns.

"Sour cream, salsa, avocado and shredded lettuce make nice toppings for these burgers."

Linda Bejaran   Turlock HS, Turlock, CA

Shrimp Ceviche

Serves: 4-6   *Central America*

1/2 head cabbage
1 bunch radishes
1 green onion, white and green parts
3-4 Roma tomatoes
1 avocado
1/2 bunch cilantro
5 limes, juice only
5-6 shakes Tapito Hot sauce
2 (3 or 4 ounce) cans bay shrimp, with canning liquid
salt and pepper, to taste

Dice all vegetables into small portions for a salsa type appearance. In a large bowl, mix all ingredients and adjust salt, pepper and hot sauce, to taste. Toss and serve on tostada shells or as a salad with corn tortilla chips.

Stephanie San Sebastian   Central HS, Fresno, CA

Apple Avocado Salsa

Serves: 4-6   *Mexico*

1 apple, diced
1 cup avocado, diced
1/4 cup red onion, diced
1 tablespoon fresh cilantro, chopped
1 1/2 teaspoons jalapeno, diced
1 garlic clove, minced
1 1/2 tablespoons fresh lime juice (or juice of 1 lime)
1/2 teaspoon lime zest
1/8 teaspoon salt
1 dash pepper

Dice apple, avocado, red onion, cilantro and chile. Mince the garlic. Squeeze the lime and zest the peel. Combine all ingredients in a bowl. Refrigerate or eat at room temperature. Eat with chips. Enjoy!

Priscilla Yazzie   Mesa HS, Mesa, AZ

Baja Fish Tacos

Serves: 4   *Mexico*

1 cup cabbage, shredded
2 tablespoons cilantro, coarsely chopped
2 tablespoons plus 3 tablespoons red salsa
salt
1/3 cup sour cream
2 cups cornmeal
3 large eggs
1 pound cod, cut crosswise into 1/2 inch thick slices
vegetable oil, for frying
8 (6 inch) soft corn tortillas
Use chipotle salsa for great smoky flavor

In a medium bowl, toss the cabbage, cilantro, 2 tablespoons salsa and salt to taste. In a small bowl, stir together the sour cream and remaining 3 tablespoons salsa. Set both aside. In a shallow dish, whisk together the cornmeal and 1 tablespoon salt. In another shallow dish, beat the eggs with a fork. Coat the fish slices in the cornmeal, then in the egg, then in the cornmeal again, and place on a plate. In a medium cast-iron or other heavy skillet, pour the oil to a depth of 1 1/2 inches and heat over medium heat until the surface ripples, about 2 minutes. Add about a third of the fish slices to the skillet and cook, turning once, until golden, 3 to 4 minutes. Transfer with a slotted spoon to a paper-towel-lined plate. Repeat with the remaining fish slices. In a large skillet, warm the tortillas on both sides over high heat. Spread about 1 teaspoon sour cream sauce on a tortilla, then top with a few pieces fish and a heaping spoonful of the slaw and fold over. Repeat with the remaining tacos.

"This is a delicious Rachel Ray 30 Minute Meals recipe. Our Foods and Nutrition class students enjoy preparing these fish tacos as part of our fish and shellfish unit. We use individually frozen haddock fillets for the fish, a readily available substitute for the cod, and also a mildly flavored fish."

Leigh Ann Diffenderfer   **Newbury Park HS, Newbury Park, CA**

Baked Beef Chimichangas

Serves: 4   *Mexico*

3/4 pound ground beef
1/4 cup chopped onion
1 clove garlic, minced
1/3 cup salsa
1 cup cheddar cheese, shredded
8 (10 inch) flour tortillas
melted butter

Preheat oven to 500 degrees. In a large skillet, cook ground beef, onion, and garlic until meat is brown and onion is tender. Drain fat. Add salsa and simmer 10 minutes, stirring occasionally. Brush both sides of flour tortillas with melted butter. Spoon meat mixture down center of each tortilla. Top each with about 2 tablespoons of cheese. Fold in the 2 sides envelope style. Place chimichangas seam side down in a greased baking dish. Bake for 8-10 minutes or until golden and crisp. To serve: set chimichangas atop lettuce and sprinkle with cheese. Serve with salsa and sour cream.

"It is one of their favorites and can be done during one class period."

Charlotte Runyan   **Saddleback HS, Santa Ana, CA**

Chicken Chili & Chips
Serves: 6   *Mexico*

1 chicken breast, cubed
1 Anaheim chile, diced
3 green onions, chopped
1 clove garlic, minced
1 Serrano, minced
3 cups milk
8 ounces cheese
3 bouillon cubes, or may use powdered bouillon or canned broth
3 tablespoons corn starch, dissolved in milk
1-2 bags chips

Sweat veggies. Add chicken and liquid ingredients, except cheese. Cook until tender and thickened. Take off stove and add cheese until melted. Enjoy over chips.

"Healthy Nachos."

Mary Morrow   **Mesa HS, Mesa, AZ**

Chicken Enchiladas
Serves: 5   *Mexico*

2 boneless, skinless chicken breasts
1 teaspoon chicken bouillon base
2 tablespoons chili powder, divided
1 tablespoon vegetable oil
1/4 onion, finely chopped
1/3 cup sour cream
1 1/4 cups grated Jack or cheddar cheese, divided
1 tablespoon chopped cilantro
1 15 (ounce) can tomato sauce
1/4 green bell pepper, finely chopped
2 whole green chiles, finely chopped
1/2 teaspoon cumin
1/2 teaspoon dried oregano
1 clove garlic, minced
5 tortillas

Preheat oven to 350 degrees. Place chicken in a medium saucepan and cover with water. Add chicken, bouillon base and 1 tablespoon chili powder. Cover and simmer on medium-low heat (don't boil) until chicken is poached. Remove chicken and place on a cutting board. Using two forks, shred chicken and place in a mixing bowl. Meanwhile, heat the vegetable oil in a small skillet. Sauté onions until translucent and soft but not brown. Combine shredded chicken with cooked onions, sour cream, 3/4 cup cheese and cilantro. Set filling aside. In a small saucepan combine the tomato sauce, 1/3 cup water, bell pepper, green chiles, remaining 1 tablespoon chili powder, cumin, oregano and garlic. Simmer over medium heat for 5 minutes. Spread 1/2 cup of sauce over the bottom of a 13 x 9 inch baking pan. Pour remaining sauce into a pie pan. Dip one tortilla in the pie pan until it is completely coated on both sides with the

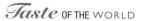

sauce. Transfer to a plate and spoon 1/5 of the chicken mixture down center of tortilla. Roll up tortilla and place in prepared baking pan. Repeat with remaining 4 tortillas and chicken mixture. Pour the remaining sauce over the enchiladas and sprinkle with the 1/2 cup cheese. Bake for 20 minutes. Garnish each enchilada with extra sour cream and chopped cilantro, if desired.

"This enchilada recipe is always a favorite of my culinary students!"

Wendy Stewart   **Oakmont High School, Roseville, CA**

Chicken Fajita Crescent Braid

Serves: 4-6   *Mexico*

2 cans Pillsbury refrigerated Crescent Dinner Rolls
2 tablespoons vegetable oil
2 large, boneless, skinless chicken breasts, cut into 1 1/2 by 1/2 inch strips
2 teaspoons chili powder
1/2 teaspoon salt
2 cloves garlic, minced
1 small white onion, thinly sliced
1 red or green bell pepper, cut into thin strips
1/2 cup Old El Paso Thick 'n Chunky Salsa (or any thick, chunky salsa)
1 cup cheddar cheese, shredded
1 cup Monterey Jack cheese, shredded
1 egg white, beaten

Preheat oven to 375 degrees. Unroll crescent rolls out onto a large baking sheet lined with parchment paper. Pinch seams together and stretch each tube of dough out to measure about 8 x 12 inches. (I've found that assembling each separate braid on a piece of parchment paper off of the baking sheet first and then moving them onto the baking sheet works best. You can bake both logs at the same time if you use a large baking sheet.) In a 12 inch skillet, heat vegetable oil over medium-high heat. Add chicken; stir in chili powder, salt and garlic; cook 3 to 5 minutes until chicken is lightly browned. Add the onion and bell pepper strips; cook 2 to 3 minutes longer or until chicken is no longer pink in the center and vegetables are crisp-tender. Spoon half the chicken mixture in a 4 inch strip down the middle of each crescent rectangle. Top each strip with half the salsa and then half the cheese. With kitchen shears, make cuts in the crescent dough on either side of the chicken mixture; similar to a zipper. Stop about an inch away from the chicken mixture. Alternately cross the strips over the filling as you braid your way down the log. Press to seal the ends of each strip down once they have been crisscrossed. Brush the tops of the logs with the beaten egg mixture. Bake 20 to 25 minutes or until deep golden brown. Cool 5 minutes before cutting crosswise into slices. Serve with salsa, sour cream and/or guacamole.

"Adapted from Pillsbury's Crescent Recipe collection. Kids love this recipe. After the first time figuring out the braiding technique, it will become a favorite of yours too!"

Beckie Bloemker   **Foothill HS, Sacramento, CA**

Chicken Fajitas

Serves: 4   ***Mexico***

1/4 cup fresh lemon juice
2 tablespoons oil
1/2 tablespoon wine vinegar
1/2 teaspoon salt
1/2 teaspoon pepper
1 teaspoon garlic powder
1 teaspoon chili powder
1 teaspoon cayenne pepper
2 chicken breasts, sliced in thin strips
1 green pepper, sliced in thin strips
1 onion, sliced in thin strips

In a bowl add lemon juice, oil, vinegar, salt, pepper, garlic powder, chili powder, and cayenne pepper and stir until combined. Add chicken strips, green peppers and onion and coat with marinade for 10 minutes or longer. In a hot, large skillet or cast iron fajita pan, add chicken, peppers and onions and cook until chicken juices run clear, about 10-15 minutes. Stir fajitas often so they don't stick to pan and burn. Serve with warm flour or corn tortillas and garnish with guacamole, cheese, and sour cream.

"I make these with my students and they all love them!"

Jill Enright   Granite Hills HS, El Cajon, CA

Chicken Posole

Serves: 4-6   ***Mexico***

3 poblano chilies about 1 pound
6 garlic cloves
1 large white onion
2 large cans (14.5 ounces each) hominy
2 pounds of boned chicken thighs or breasts skinned
1/2 teaspoon salt
2 teaspoons Mexican oregano
2 tablespoons olive oil
3 cups chicken broth
3 tablespoons red New Mexico chili powder
sliced avocado, lime wedges, cilantro springs, and sour cream

Preheat broiler and cook poblanos on a baking sheet until dark on both sides. Finely chop garlic, then the onion and combine. Cut chicken into 1 to 2 inch pieces and season with salt and oregano. Heat oil in a big pan and brown, turning every couple of minutes until brown. Remove chicken and place onion and garlic mixture into pan and saute until softened about 5 minutes. Combine all ingredients into a large pan, bring to a boil, then let simmer for about an hour. Top the soup with avocado, lime, and sour cream before serving.

"Nice served with warm tortillas!"

Lisa Washmuth   San Luis Obispo HS, San Luis Obispo, CA

Chilaquiles

Serves: 8   *Mexico*

1 dozen corn tortillas, cut in strips, fried in olive oil
1 tablespoon olive oil
1 small (14.5 ounce) can whole tomatoes, chopped
1 small can of Oretega green chili
1 medium yellow onion, chopped
1/4 teaspoon chili powder, to taste
1 teaspoon salt
1/4 teaspoon cumin
1 (16 ounce) container sour cream
1 cup cheddar cheese, shredded
1 cup Jack cheese, shredded

Preheat oven to 350 degrees. Line the bottom of a 9 x 13 inch baking dish with tortilla strips that have been fried in olive oil. Prepare sauce. Sauté with 1 tablespoon olive oil, chopped tomatoes, chili and onion. Sprinkle in chili powder, salt, and cumin. Let simmer approximately 10 minutes. Pour sour cream and mixed cheese over layers of tortillas. Pour sauce over each layer. End with cheese on top. Bake at 350 degrees for 20 minutes.

"Fun, fast family recipe."

Patricia Lind   Bear River HS, Grass Valley, CA

Chipotle Chicken and Avocado Quesadilla

Serves: 6   *Mexico*

1 1/2 cups roasted chicken, shredded
3/4 cup canned black beans, drained and rinsed
1/2 bunch green onion, thinly sliced
1/4 cup cilantro, roughly chopped
2 tablespoons canned chipotle chile, minced
2 tablespoons red wine vinegar
1 tablespoon olive oil
1/2 teaspoon salt
1/4 teaspoon black pepper
6 ounces grated Mexican cheese blend (manchego, panela, cotija)
6 10-inch flour tortillas
softened butter
1 fresh avocado, cut into 1/4-inch slices

Combine chicken, black beans, onions, cilantro, chile, vinegar, oil, salt and pepper in a mixing bowl. Let stand 20 minutes to blend flavors. Lay tortillas on a plate and brush with soft or melted butter. Place a large skillet over medium-high heat. Place tortilla, buttered side down, into the skillet and place a portion of cheese mixture over entire tortilla. Place a portion of chicken mixture over half of the tortilla, leaving the other half empty. Cover chicken mixture with a few avocado slices. Cook until cheese begins to melt, about 3 to 4 minutes. Fold tortilla in half, over the avocado and chicken mixture. Continue cooking until tortilla is lightly golden on both sides and cheese begins to ooze. Repeat with remaining quesadillas. Cut each into wedges to serve.

"This recipe came from the famous Too Hot Tamales, *by Mary Sue Milliken and Susan Feniger. For great Mexican food, they cannot be beat!"*

Margo Olsen   Amador Valley and Foothill HS, Pleasanton, CA

Enchilada Verde
Serves: 6   **Mexico**

1 large can green enchilada sauce
cooking oil
1 dozen corn tortillas
2 (8 ounce) packages cream cheese, softened
3-4 green onions, chopped
4 chicken breasts, cooked and shredded
Monterey Jack cheese, shredded

Preheat oven to 350 degrees. Warm enchilada sauce in small frying pan. Heat approximately 1 inch oil in separate frying pan. Heat until bubbles form around dipped tortilla. Quickly dip tortilla in oil on both sides. Stack between paper towels. Combine cream cheese, onions and chicken in a bowl and set aside. Dip one tortilla in sauce, lay in 9 X 12 baking dish, put about 3 tablespoons of the cream cheese/chicken mixture in the tortilla, roll and place in dish seam side down. Continue until all twelve enchiladas are assembled in dish. Top with remaining green sauce. Top with desired amount Monterey Jack cheese. Bake approximately 45 minutes. Serve with sour cream.

"A friend gave me this recipe and everyone loves it!"

Sue Campbell   **Marsh JHS, Chico, CA**

Grandma's Salsa Verde
Serves: 6   **Mexico**

16 Anaheim green chiles
2 habanero chiles
1 whole garlic head
1 to 2 (28 ounce) cans whole stewed tomatoes
salt to taste

Using a torch or gas stove top, roast chiles until skin turns black. Under running water, remove skins from chiles. Mash garlic cloves. Put all ingredients into blender and mix until evenly blended.

"A family recipe passed down for generations. Great on eggs, chips, virtually anything!"

Renee Pelkey   **Huntington Beach HS, Huntington Beach, CA**

Homemade Tortillas
Makes: 8   **Mexico**

2 cups all purpose flour
1/2 teaspoon salt
1 cup water
3 tablespoons olive oil

Combine flour and salt. Stir in water and oil. On a floured surface, knead 5-6 times. Divide dough into 8 portions. On a lightly floured surface, roll each portion into a 7 inch circle. On a nonstick skillet coated with cooking spray, cook tortillas over medium heat for I minute on each side or until lightly browned.

"For years I have longed for my Grama's homemade tortillas, I saw this quick and easy recipe in Taste of Home and they are the closest to Grama's that I've found. Very easy too."

Robin Ali   **Nevada Union HS, Grass Valley, CA**

Mexican Bread Pudding

Serves: 24   **Mexico**

5 cups water
5 1/3 cups brown sugar
12 cinnamon sticks
20 cups French bread, cubed
1 cup sliced almonds
1 1/3 cups raisins
1 cup butter
2 cups Monterey Jack cheese

Combine water, brown sugar and cinnamon sticks in a saucepan and simmer for 15 minutes. Remove cinnamon sticks and discard. Combine bread, almonds, raisins and butter and mix well. Pour sugar mixture over bread mixture and mix. Spray two 9 x 13 inch baking pans with cooking spray and place mixture in pans. Chill for 1 hour and remove. Top with Monterey Jack cheese, cover with foil and bake for 25 minutes at 350 degrees. Remove foil and bake an additional 10 minutes. Serve warm.

"My family and students love this bread pudding, serve with vanilla ice cream! A recipe I got from Kathy Ewing, a retired home economics teacher from Modesto who was a frequent contributor to California Cookbooks. I submit this recipe in her honor."

Linda Johnson   **Enochs HS, Modesto, CA**

Mexican Chicken

Serves: 8-12   **Mexico**

8 corn tortillas
4 cups cooked boneless chicken
1 (10.5 ounce) can cream of tomato soup
1 (10.5 ounce) can cream of chicken soup
1 (4 ounce) can diced green chile peppers
2 cups cheddar cheese, grated

Preheat oven to 350 degrees. Spray a 9 x 13 inch casserole pan. Cut tortillas into 1/8 wedges and layer tortilla wedges on bottom of pan. Spread cooked bite size chicken pieces on top of tortillas. Combine tomato soup, chicken soup and chiles; pour over chicken. Top with grated cheddar cheese. Bake about 30 minutes until bubbly and heated throughout.

"Spice this casserole up with your choice of diced chiles. Excellent dish for potlucks."

Neva Clausen   **Lebanon HS, Lebanon, OR**

Mexican Wedding Cookies

Makes: 35 cookies   **Mexico**

3/4 cup pecans
2 cups all-purpose flour, divided
1/2 cup powdered sugar
1 cup butter, slightly softened
1 teaspoon vanilla extract
1/2 teaspoon almond extract
1 cup powdered sugar for rolling cookies

Preheat the oven to 350 degrees. Place the pecans in the bowl of a food processor along with one cup of the flour. Using on and off pulsations, grind together until nuts are fine. Beat the sugar with the butter. The butter should not be too soft or the cookie dough will be difficult to work with. Add the extracts. Add the nut-flour mixture to the butter. Beat in the remaining cup of flour. Refrigerate the cookie dough for 20 minutes. Form the batter into balls and place on ungreased baking sheets. Bake for 12 minutes. When they have cooled for about 15 minutes, sprinkle powdered sugar over the tops until they are completely covered.

"These cookies are a traditional cookie of Mexico, found at every panaderia in the small villages or the elegant bakeries of Mexico City!"

Cheryl Whittington   Saddleback HS, Santa Ana, CA

Mrs. Fuxa's Shrimp Enchiladas
Makes: 10-12   *Mexico*

2 tablespoons green onion, chopped
1 teaspoon garlic, minced
2-3 tablespoons taco seasoning
1 tablespoon water
16 ounces (1 pound) bay shrimp, cooked
1/2 cup tomato, chopped or salsa
1/4 cup sour cream
1 (28 ounce) can La Victoria mild green enchilada sauce
2 cups Colby and Monterey Jack cheese mix, shredded
12 (8 inch) flour tortillas

Sauté green onion and garlic over low heat in a large skillet with 1 tablespoon oil. Add taco seasoning with water and stir until dissolved. Add shrimp and tomatoes, simmer about 2 minutes. Add sour cream, stir until heated through. Remove from heat. Let stand for 5 minutes. Preheat oven to 350 degrees. In a 13 x 9 inch pan, pour just enough sauce to cover the bottom of the pan. Take 1 tortilla at a time and cover both sides with sauce. Place wet tortilla in the pan and put 1-2 tablespoons of shrimp mixture and sprinkle with cheese. Roll the tortilla and place the seam side down. Repeat with remaining tortillas. Use remaining cheese to sprinkle on the top of the enchiladas. Cover with foil and bake 25-30 minutes or until cheese is melted.

Lori Fuxa   Rancho Alamitos HS, Garden Grove,

Muffy's Marvelous Mexican Chimes
Serves: 6-8   *Mexico*

2 pounds meat (pork, beef or chicken)
1 teaspoon garlic salt
1 teaspoon onion salt
1 teaspoon chili powder
1 teaspoon oregano
2 teaspoons cumin
1 teaspoon paprika
1 teaspoon seasoning salt
1 teaspoon pepper
2 teaspoons Mexican seasoning
2 teaspoons Accent
2 cups Monterey Jack cheese, grated

Combine spices. Sprinkle over meat, marinate overnight in an airtight container. Cook in a crock pot slowly for 6-8 hours. Shred meat with a fork. Add cheese. Fill flour tortillas. Roll up and fry in hot oil.
"Napoleon Dynamite would have loved these!"

Julie Ericksen   Skyline HS, Salt Lake City, UT

Natalie's Quick Chicken Mole

Serves: 4   *Mexico*

1 teaspoon salt
1 teaspoon pepper
1 teaspoon garlic powder
1 bay leaf
6-8 chicken thighs
2 cups water
1 whole round Mexican chocolate (such as Abuelita brand)
1 (8.25 ounces) jar mole (find in Mexican aisle of grocery store)
1 tablespoon creamy peanut butter

Combine salt, pepper and garlic powder; use mixture to season chicken pieces. Cook chicken in skillet along with bay leaf until done, about 10-15 minutes, turning once. In separate pot, combine remaining ingredients and cook on low heat until melted and smooth, stirring as needed. Add a little water if mixture is too thick, being careful not to make sauce too runny. Add chicken (remove skin if desired) to mole mixture and simmer about 7 minutes, stirring regularly. Enjoy mole served with Mexican rice and beans.
"Natalie works at several Turlock schools by day and enjoys preparing Mexican foods for a local grocery store in the afternoon and evenings so that many can taste family-inspired authentic Mexican foods at home."

Laura de la Motte   Turlock HS, Turlock, CA

Ranchero Beans

Makes: 1 large pot   *Mexico*

1 1/2 pounds pinto beans
1 pound bacon, fried and chopped (reserve grease)
1 bunch green onions, chopped
3 Roma tomatoes, chopped
4-6 Serrano chiles, diced
1 bunch cilantro, chopped fine
2-3 tablespoons chicken bouillon

Wash beans, put in a large saucepan and cover with water. Bring to a boil, simmer 2-3 hours or until beans are soft. While beans are cooking, fry the bacon. When bacon is done, crumble and set aside. In the bacon grease, cook onion, tomatoes, and Serrano chiles. When soft, add bacon and cilantro. When beans are done, add all tomato mixture. Stir in bouillon. Cover and cook 10 minutes.
"I got this recipe from Adela Centeno, a dear friend who was kind enough to share this awesome recipe."

Cari Sheridan   Grace Yokley MS, Ontario, CA

Rice Pudding (Arroz con Leche)

Makes: 10   **Mexico**

    5 quarts of water
    1 1/2 cups long grain white rice (unconverted)
    1 1/2 quarts milk (warm)
    3 cups evaporated milk
    2 cups sugar
    2 sticks cinnamon, about 3-4 inches long
    1/2 cup raisins
    cinnamon powder, to taste

In a medium sauce pan, boil 2 quarts of water and add the rice. Stir rice and remove from the heat. Let the rice soak for 25 minutes. Rinse the rice using a hand strainer and drain excess water. Set aside. In another sauce pan, boil the 3 quarts of water and add the rice. Boil the rice uncovered for about 30 minutes until the rice is soft and tender. Do not overcook, and remove excess water. Set aside. Mix the warm milk, evaporated milk, sugar and cinnamon sticks in a medium sauce pan. Cook for approximately 45 minutes until the liquids begin to get thick, and slowly change in color. Add the cooked rice and raisins and cook for another 45 minutes or until the rice pudding thickens. Remove from heat and stir every so often until the rice cools. Serve the rice on a platter or individual bowls and sprinkle with cinnamon powder.

"My mother used to make this fabulous recipe during the Christmas season, or on a cold winter night growing up in Chicago."

Elvia Nieto   **Alhambra HS, Alhambra, CA**

Simple and Perfect Enchiladas

Serves: 6   **Mexico**

    1 tablespoon canola oil
    1 tablespoon flour
    1 (28 ounce) can enchilada sauce
    2 cups chicken stock or broth
    1/2 teaspoon salt
    1/2 teaspoon ground black pepper
    2 tablespoons chopped cilantro
    1 1/2 pounds ground beef
    1 medium onion, diced
    2 (4 ounce) cans diced green chilies
    1/2 teaspoon salt
    12 whole corn tortillas
    1/2 cup canola oil
    3 cups sharp cheddar cheese, grated
    1/2 cup cilantro, chopped

Preheat oven to 350 degrees. In a medium sauce pan over medium heat, combine oil and flour, whisk to make a smooth paste, cook one minute. Add sauce, stock, salt, pepper, and cilantro. Bring to a boil, then reduce heat and simmer 30-45 minutes. In a skillet, brown the meat and the onions, drain any extra fat. Stir in green chiles and salt. Heat oil in a small frying pan over medium heat. One by one, using tongs, fry tortillas in oil, until soft, not crisp, about 30 seconds per side. Remove and drain on paper towels. Repeat until all tortillas have been fried. Pour 1/2 cup sauce in bottom of baking pan, spread to cover. Dip each tortilla in sauce, then spoon in a little meat and

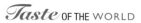

cheese. Roll up and place seam down in pan. Repeat until all tortillas are filled and pan is full. Pour extra sauce over and sprinkle with remaining cheese. Bake for 20 minutes or until bubbly. Sprinkle cilantro on before serving.

"So worth the time!"

Shauna Young   **Jordan HS, Sandy, Utah**

Sopapillas
Makes: 2 dozen   *Mexico*

4 cups all-purpose flour
2 teaspoons baking powder
1 teaspoon salt
4 tablespoons shortening
1 1/2 cups warm water
2 quarts oil for frying

In a large bowl, stir together flour, baking powder, salt and shortening. Stir in water; mix until dough is smooth. Cover and let stand for 20 minutes. Roll out on floured board until 1/8 to 1/4 inch thick. Cut into 3 inch squares. Heat oil in deep-fryer to 375 degrees. Fry until golden brown on both sides. Drain on paper towels and serve hot with honey.

"I first had these when I went to visit my sister in New Mexico. My nephews taught me the trick of poking a hole in the sopapilla and filling it with honey. Whenever I have sopapillas I always think of Jeff, Mitchell and Tristan."

Shasta Jolly   **Villa Park HS, Villa Park, CA**

Spicy Mexican Chicken Lasagna
Serves: 6-8   *Mexico*

2 roasted yellow peppers, cut into strips (I've also used red)
1 cup green salsa
9 no boil lasagna sheets
1 cup light sour cream
1 cup milk
1 egg
2 teaspoons flour
2 cups chicken, cooked and shredded
2 cups fresh cilantro (or to taste)
1 1/2 cups Monterey Jack cheese, shredded
1 (15 ounce) can corn (you could also use frozen)

Preheat oven to 350 degrees. Use a 13 x 9 x 2 inch pan. Spread 1/2 cup salsa in pan. Top with 3 noodles, leaving 1 inch between. Whisk sour cream, milk, egg, and flour until blended (sauce will be thin). Pour 2/3 cup sauce over noodles. Scatter 2 cups cooked, shredded chicken on top. Sprinkle with 1/4 cup cilantro and 1/2 cup Monterey Jack cheese. Dot with 2 tablespoons salsa. Cover with 3 more noodles and 2/3 cup sauce. Top with peppers, 1/2 cup cheese, corn, and 1/4 cup cilantro. Top with 3 more noodles, remaining sauce, salsa, and cheese. Cover with foil. Bake 40-45 minutes. Let stand 10 minutes. Cover with remaining cilantro (if desired).

Sue Campbell   **Marsh JHS, Chico, CA**

Stacked Tacos

Serves: 4   *Mexico*

1 (15 ounce) can chili, no beans
2 (15 ounce) cans chili, with beans
8 corn tortillas
1 cup cheddar cheese, grated
1 (1 ounce) bag Lays Potato Chips

Preheat oven to 350 degrees. Mix all three cans of chili together in a small bowl. In a casserole dish sprayed with cooking spray, alternate layers of corn tortillas (using 4 the first time), chili and cheese. Repeat layer again using remaining 4 tortillas, chili and cheese. Top with potato chips and bake for 30 minutes.

Deanna Lee   Marina HS, Huntington Beach, CA

Taco Casserole

Serves: 4   *Mexico*

1 pound ground beef
1/2 onion, chopped
1 clove garlic, chopped
1 (1 ounce) package taco seasoning
corn chips
Jack cheese, shredded
2 tomatoes, chopped
sour cream, optional
lettuce, optional

Preheat oven to 350 degrees. In skillet, brown ground beef, adding onion and garlic until well done. Add seasoning packet, stir well. In 8 x inch 8 baking dish, place a layer of broken corn chips. Add 1/2 of beef mixture, then add layers of cheese and tomatoes. Repeat the layers 1 more time. Bake for 30 minutes. Before serving, top with a spoonful of sour cream and serve lettuce on the side.

"Got this recipe from a friend of mine that has retired from teaching. She has served this for many years. It is quick to prepare, ingredients are usually on hand at home, and it is a less messy way to enjoy tacos."

Sharon Both   Gladstone HS, Covina, CA

Tacos Picadillo Pico de Gallo

Serves: 6   *Mexico*

12 flour or corn Tortillas
1 cup cheese, shredded (cheddar or Jack)
2 cups iceberg lettuce, thinly shredded
Picadillo (Mexican Ground Beef Mixture):
1 pound ground beef
1 tablespoon garlic, minced
1/2 cup onion, finely chopped
1/2 cup bell pepper, finely chopped
1/2 cup tomatoes, finely chopped
1/2 cup celery, finely chopped
1 teaspoon oregano
1 1/2 teaspoons beef base
1 teaspoon black pepper
1 teaspoon cumin
1/2 bay leaf
salt and pepper, to taste
Pico de Gallo (Tomato Salsa):
1 1/2 cups tomatoes, small dice
1/4 cup red onions, small dice
1 tablespoon cilantro, minced
1 teaspoon jalapeno, minced
2 teaspoons lime juice
1/2 teaspoon salt
pinch black pepper
Lime Sour Cream:
1/4 cup sour cream
1 1/2 teaspoons lime juice
1/4 teaspoon salt
1/2 teaspoon jalapeno, minced
2 tablespoons milk

Picadillo: Place ground beef and garlic in skillet and cook for about 15 minutes or until beef is browned. Break beef into small pieces as it cooks. Strain some of the excess liquid. Add the rest of the ingredients and cook for 5 minutes or until the veggies are cooked, stirring occasionally. Remove bay leaf. Taste and adjust seasonings. Should be flavorful! Veggies should be bright in color; beef should be finely crumbled and moist!
Pico de Gallo (Tomato Salsa): Mix all ingredients together. Taste and adjust seasonings.
Lime Sour Cream: Mix all ingredients in mixing bowl. Taste and adjust seasonings.
Tacos: Fill flour or corn tortilla with Picadillo mixture. Sprinkle with cheese, then lettuce, then Pico de Gallo, and top with Lime Sour Cream.

Pat Freshour   **Foothill HS, Palo Cedro, CA**

The Best Chile Relleno Casserole

Serves: 6-8   *Mexico*

1 pound Jack cheese, grated
1 pound cheddar cheese, grated
2 (4 ounce) cans green chiles
4 egg whites
4 egg yolks
2/3 cup evaporated milk
1 tablespoon flour
1/4 teaspoon salt
1/2 teaspoon pepper
2 medium tomatoes, sliced

Preheat oven to 325 degrees. Combine cheese and chilies in a large bowl then turn out into a greased 9 x 13 baking pan. Beat egg whites until stiff. Mix yolks, evaporated milk, flour, salt and pepper until well blended. Fold the yolks mixture into the egg whites. Pour over cheese and mix in slightly with a fork. Bake for 30 minutes. Top with tomatoes and bake another 30 minutes.

"A family favorite for years and is reported to be John Wayne's favorite casserole."
Tisha Ludeman   **Brookhurst JHS, Anaheim, CA**

Tortilla Soup

Serves: 4   *Mexico*

1 small onion, chopped
2 tablespoons vegetable oil
2 1/2 cups canned tomatoes, chopped
3 cups chicken broth
1 (4 ounce) can Ortega chile, chopped
1/2 teaspoon cumin
1 teaspoon salt
1/4 teaspoon pepper
1/2 cup cilantro
1 cup cooked, shredded chicken
1/2 cup corn (fresh or frozen)
1 cup cheddar cheese, grated
2 cups tortilla strips (corn)

Saute onion in oil until soft. Add tomatoes, chicken broth, chile, cumin, salt, pepper and cilantro. Cook 10 minutes. Add chicken and corn; simmer 5 minutes. To serve: place some tortilla chips in each bowl. Ladle soup over chips. Sprinkle with cheese and cilantro. Garnish with sour cream and lime wedges.

"It is our family tradition to share this soup on Christmas Eve with family and friends."
Charlotte Runyan   **Saddleback HS, Santa Ana, CA**

Vegan Taco Meat

Serves: 4   *Mexico*

1 package Yves Vegie Cuisine meatless ground
1 tablespoon taco seasoning mix
1/2 package Soy Chorizo

Continued on page 66

Chile Verde de Puerco

Serves: 8   *Mexico*

3 pounds boneless pork shoulder, or country-style ribs, cut into 1 1/2-inch pieces
1 teaspoon salt
1 teaspoon black pepper
4-6 tablespoons flour
5 tablespoons vegetable oil, divided
2 large onions, diced
8 cloves garlic, crushed
2 pounds tomatillos, husked, cored and quartered
1 tablespoon ground cumin
1 tablespoon dried oregano
1 cinnamon stick
1 12-oz can beer
1 14 1/2-oz can chicken broth
6 poblano chiles, halved, seeded, sliced into 1/2-inch thick strips
2 yellow bell peppers, seeded and cut into 1-inch squares
3/4 cup cilantro, chopped
2 teaspoons orange zest, grated

Season pork with salt and pepper; dust with flour. Heat 4 tablespoons oil in Dutch oven, brown pork in batches, transferring pork to bowl when browned. Heat remaining tablespoon oil in pot. Add onion, sauté 3-4 minutes, until soft, stir in garlic and sauté one minute more. Add tomatillos, cumin, oregano, cinnamon and pork. Add beer and broth; bring to a boil, lower heat and simmer, partially covered, 2 hours, stirring occasionally. Add chiles and yellow pepper, simmer partially covered for 30-45 minutes more, until chiles are tender. Discard cinnamon stick. Stir in cilantro and orange zest.

National Pork Board   **PorkBeInspired.com**

Mango Chiles Rellenos

Serves: 6   *Mexico*

6 large poblano or Anaheim peppers
1/2 medium white onion, peeled and cut into rings
2 ripe mangos, peeled, pitted and sliced, divided
6 ounces jack cheese, cut into 12 strips
1 tablespoon lime juice
1 very small chipotle pepper
1 teaspoon adobo sauce from can
Snipped fresh cilantro

Grill peppers and onions over high heat until peppers are well charred and onion is lightly charred. Place peppers in paper bag and fold top over several times; set aside for 20 minutes. Remove peels from peppers by rubbing gently with fingers. Make a slit the length of each pepper and carefully remove seeds and membranes. Place 2 large mango slices and 2 cheese strips inside each pepper. Place on large piece of heavy duty foil and grill over medium heat for 5 to 10 minutes, or until cheese is melted. Remove from grill and keep warm. Chop 1/2 cup mango. Puree grilled onions, remaining mango, lime juice, chipotle peppers and adobo sauce until smooth. Season to taste with salt and stir in chopped mango. Place small amount of mango salsa on each serving plate and top each relleno with additional salsa and snipped cilantro.

Chile Verde de Puerco

Mango Chiles Rellenos

Salmon with Wisconsin Parmesan Horseradish Crust & Dijon Cream

Pacific Rim Chicken Burgers with Ginger Mayonnaise

Salmon with Wisconsin Parmesan Horseradish Crust & Dijon Cream

Serves: 6   *USA*

Salmon
1 1/2 cups Italian-seasoned dry breadcrumbs
1 cup (about 4 ounces) Wisconsin Parmesan Cheese, grated
1/2 cup prepared horseradish
2 tablespoons olive oil
2 teaspoons dry Cajun seasoning mixture
6 salmon fillets (6-8 ounces each)
Dijon Cream:
1 1/2 cups heavy cream
1 1/2 tablespoons Dijon mustard
Salt and ground white pepper
For the salmon, preheat oven to 400°F

> Wisconsin Milk
> Marketing Board
> WisDairy.com

In bowl, combine breadcrumbs, cheese, horseradish, olive oil, and seasoning; mix well. Pat 1/2 cup of seasoned crumb mixture on top of each salmon fillet to completely cover the top. Roast crusted fillets for 15 to 18 minutes or until cooked through. While salmon is cooking, prepare Dijon cream. In heavy saucepan, cook cream over low heat until it reduces to approximately 3/4 cup. Stir in mustard and season with salt and white pepper. Serve each fillet with 2 tablespoons of the Dijon cream.

Pacific Rim Chicken Burgers with Ginger Mayonnaise

> National Chicken Council

Serves: 4   *Japan*

1 1/4 pounds ground chicken
2/3 cup panko
  (Japanese bread crumbs)
1 egg, lightly beaten
2 green onions, thinly sliced
3 tablespoons chopped cilantro
1 clove garlic, minced
1 teaspoon Asian hot chili sauce
1 teaspoon salt
1 tablespoon vegetable oil
1/2 cup bottled teriyaki glaze
4 teaspoons honey
4 sesame buns, split and toasted

4 leaves red lettuce
1 cucumber, peeled, seeded,
  halved and thinly
sliced lengthwise
Ginger Mayonnaise:
1/2 cup mayonnaise
2 teaspoons sweet pickle relish
2 teaspoons minced fresh ginger
2 teaspoons lime juice
1 clove garlic (minced)
1/4 teaspoon salt
cilantro sprigs

In large bowl, mix together chicken, panko, egg, onions, cilantro, garlic, chili sauce and salt. With oiled hands, form into 4 patties. In small bowl, mix together teriyaki glaze and honey. In large non-stick fry pan over medium high heat, place oil. Add chicken and cook, turning and brushing with teriyaki glaze, about 10 minutes or until done. Place burgers on toasted buns and top with lettuce, cucumber and Ginger Mayonnaise. Garnish with additional cilantro and cucumber slices. Ginger Mayonnaise: In small bowl, mix together mayonnaise, sweet pickle relish, minced fresh ginger, lime juice, minced garlic and teaspoon salt.

Empty the meatless ground in a large skillet. Add the taco seasoning mix. Add the Soy Chorizo. Make sure that you take it out of the plastic casing. Heat just until warm. Do not overcook.

"Trader Joes, Whole Foods, or health food stores have these. It's healthier and you won't miss the beef. A good vegan "cheese" to use with the tacos is Daiya Cheddar Style Shreds. This "cheese" is made, believe it or not, with tapioca and is dairy and soy free."

Janet Tingley   Atascadero HS, Atascadero, CA

Vegetable Enchiladas

Makes: 8   *Mexico*

1 tablespoon olive oil
1/4 cup red onion, diced
1/8 teaspoon salt
1/4 teaspoon chili powder
1/2 teaspoon ground cumin
1 1/2 teaspoons garlic, minced
1/2 red bell pepper, chopped
1/2 Italian squash, sliced
3 mushrooms, sliced
1/2 cup corn
1/2 cup black beans, drained and rinsed
2 tablespoons salsa
8 flour tortillas
2 cups green enchilada sauce
1 cup Jack or cheddar cheese, shredded
2 tablespoons cilantro, for garnish
avocado slices, for garnish

In a large skillet over medium heat: add oil and sauté the red onion, garlic and spices until onion is soft. Add bell pepper and Italian squash, cook for 3 minutes. Add the mushrooms, corn and beans. Cook for another 5 minutes until the mushrooms are soft and the corn is crisp tender. Remove from heat. Stir in salsa. Preheat oven to 375 degrees. Place 1/4 cup green sauce in the bottom of a 9 x 13 inch baking dish. Place remaining sauce in a pie pan. Dip tortilla in green sauce making sure to coat both sides. Spoon 3 tablespoons of the filling into tortilla and then sprinkle with 1 tablespoon cheese. Roll the tortilla up and place seam side down in the baking pan. Repeat with remaining tortillas. Sprinkle with remaining cheese. Cover with foil and bake 20 minutes or until the cheese is melted and bubbly. Remove from oven and sprinkle with cilantro. Serve with avocado slices on top.

Lori Fuxa   Rancho Alamitos HS, Garden Grove, CA

Watermelon Agua Fresca

Serves: 6   *Mexico*

1 small seedless watermelon
2 quarts water
1 cup lime juice
1 cup sugar
ice

Cut the red part of melon away from the white and the rind. Keep only the ripely pink meat of the melon. Pick out any errant seeds. Cut the melon into chunks. Puree half of the chunks and finely chop the rest. Put all the puree and the chopped melon into a jar. Add the water, lime juice, and sugar. Stir well till sugar dissolves. Serve well chilled over ice.

"Refreshing summer drink!"

Val Logie   Ladera Ranch MS, Ladera Ranch, CA

Lomo Saltado

Serves: 6   *Peru*

    oil, enough to cover bottom of skillet
    1 pound beef sirloin, cut into 1-1/2 inch long strips
    2 medium onions, cut into eighths
    4 tomatoes, cut into eighths
    2 tablespoons cilantro or Italian parsley, chopped
    1 tablespoon balsamic vinegar
    1/2 teaspoon lemon juice
    salt and pepper to taste
    1 pound French fries, freshly made

Heat the oil in a large skillet or wok over high heat; add beef and stir fry until beef is seared on all sides, but not fully cooked. Remove beef, with the juices and set aside. Lower heat to medium-high setting and add some fresh oil to pan. Add onions and sauté until they soften (about 2 minutes). Add tomatoes, some cilantro, soy sauce, vinegar, salt and pepper. Cook until tomatoes have softened (about 2 minutes). Add lemon juice. Add beef and toss gently. Adjust seasonings. Add French Fries and toss gently. Serve with steamed white rice. Enjoy!

"This recipe was given to me by one of my students from my International Foods class. It's a class favorite and I have become a fan of Peruvian foods."

Diane Villa   Downey HS, Downey, CA

Quinoa and Black Beans

Serves: 6   *Peru*

    1/2 teaspoon vegetable oil
    1/2 onion, chopped
    1 1/2 cloves garlic, peeled and chopped
    1/2 cup uncooked quinoa
    3/4 cup vegetable broth
    1/2 teaspoon ground cumin
    1/8 teaspoon cayenne pepper
    salt and pepper, to taste
    1/2 cup frozen corn kernels
    1 (15 ounce) can black beans, rinsed and drained
    1/4 cup fresh cilantro, chopped (optional)

Heat the oil in a medium saucepan over medium heat. Stir in the onion and garlic, and sauté until lightly browned. Mix quinoa into the saucepan and cover with vegetable broth. Season with cumin, cayenne pepper, salt and pepper. Bring mixture to a boil. Cover, reduce heat, and simmer for 20 minutes. Stir frozen corn into the saucepan and continue to simmer about 5 minutes until heated through. Mix in the black beans and cilantro.

Patty Bulat   Rogers MS, Long Beach, CA

Empanadas De Dulce (Sweet Turnovers)

Makes: 12-15   *South America*

Apricot filling:
12 ounces fresh apricots (3 cups), pitted and quartered
  (can substitute equal amount of canned pineapple tidbits, drained
  and tossed with fresh unsweetened coconut)
1/2 cup water (for the apricots)
1 fresh lemon
2/3 cup sugar
2 tablespoons water (for the cornstarch)
1 tablespoon cornstarch
1 teaspoon cinnamon
Dough:
2 cups flour
1 teaspoon salt
2/3 cup shortening
5-7 tablespoons cold water
1/4 cup powdered sugar for dusting finished empanadas

Preheat oven to 375 degrees. *Apricot filling:* Wash, pit and chop apricots. Place in medium saucepan along with the 1/2 cup water. Add lemon juice squeezed from both sides of a cut lemon and the sugar. Stir to combine. Heat on low, stirring to prevent sugar from burning. Meanwhile stir water into cornstarch and cinnamon. Stir to dissolve. Set aside. Continue cooking apricots for 2-3 minutes, stirring constantly on medium heat. When slightly softened add cornstarch mixture. Stir and watch it until it appears thickened. Remove from heat to cool. This is your filling for the empanadas. *Empanadas:* Combine flour and salt in a large mixing bowl. With a pastry blender, cut in shortening. Mixture should be fairly coarse. Sprinkle with water, one tablespoon at a time. Toss with a fork after each addition. Mix lightly until all flour is moistened and dough almost cleans the sides of the bowl. Gather together with hands; press firmly into a ball. Flour board and roll out as if for pie crust. Cut into 4 inch circles using empty cup. Spoon 1 tablespoon filling on one side, fold over and pinch closed. Bake for 15 minutes or until brown. Dust with powdered sugar while still warm.

"This filling is one I created to take advantage of local fresh fruits. Also great with peaches, or plums. A more traditional filling would be made with pumpkin, raisins or pineapple substitution listed above. My students love these!"

Patti Bartholomew   **Casa Roble HS, Orangevale, California**

Europe

· ·

Dolma (Armenian Stuffed Vegetables)

Serves: 4-6   *Armenia*

choice of fresh vegetables (green bell peppers, zucchini, eggplant, etc.)
1 1/4 pound ground lamb (ground beef can be substituted)
2/3 cup instant rice (or pre-cooked rice)
1/4 cup fresh parsley, chopped
3/4 to 1 cup yellow onion, chopped
salt and pepper, to taste
3 (8 ounce) cans tomato sauce

Preheat oven to 350 degrees. Prepare vegetables by washing and cleaning thoroughly. Cut the tops off of the bell peppers, pull out the core and seeds. Cut zucchini and long eggplant lengthwise, and scoop out the fleshy part of the squash, leaving about 3/8 inch around the edge of the zucchini and/or eggplant. Save the scooped out squash for use later on. Prepare the filling by placing the ground lamb, rice, parsley, salt and pepper in a medium bowl. Use about 2/3 of one can of tomato sauce for the filling, and mix with your hands like a meat loaf mixture. Fill each vegetable with the meat filling. For the eggplant and zucchini, layer the scooped out squash flesh on top of the filled shells, and cover with a small amount of tomato sauce. Pour additional sauce on the bottom of your baking dish around each piece. Cover with a tight fitting lid or foil for baking. Bake for 40 minutes (or more) for the squash and eggplant; 1 hour for the peppers. Check the filling for doneness in the center, especially for the peppers.

"Great way to use fresh summer vegetables. Make ahead and freeze for a quick meal."

Laurel Haley   Fresno HS, Fresno, CA

English Cream Scones

Serves: 8   *England*

2 cups flour
1/2 cup butter
1 tablespoon baking powder
1/4 cup currants
2 tablespoons sugar
2/3 cup milk, plus extra for brushing tops
1/4 teaspoon salt
Turbinado sugar (raw sugar)

Preheat oven to 450 degrees. In mixing bowl, stir together flour, baking powder, sugar and salt. Cut in butter until crumbly and pieces are the size of small peas. Stir in currants. Stir in milk until the mixture forms a ball. Roll or pat on a floured surface to a 9 inch circle. Cut into 8 wedges. Place on baking sheet. Brush tops with milk and sprinkle with turbinado sugar. Bake for 10-12 minutes or until lightly browned. Serve with Devonshire cream and jam.

"Always a class favorite."

Joy Aiello   Porterville HS, Porterville, CA

Sticky Toffee Pudding

Serves: 4-6   *England*

Pudding:
8 ounces dates
8 ounces sugar
8 ounces flour
3 ounces margarine
2 eggs
1/2 teaspoon bicarbonate of soda
Topping:
small carton heavy cream
4 ounces butter
4 ounces brown sugar

Preheat oven to 350 degrees. Soak dates in 8 ounces boiling water. Mix pudding ingredients. Add dates and stir. Pour into deep baking stone. Bake about 45 minutes. Topping: Melt butter and brown sugar in pan over low heat. Add cream until it thickens. Pour evenly over pudding. May be served with ice cream.

Julia Roman   Pacifica HS, Garden Grove, CA

Warm Brownie Pudding Cake

Serves: 6-8   *England*

3/4 cup flour
3/4 cup sugar
1 1/2 teaspoons baking powder
1/2 teaspoon baking soda
1/4 teaspoon salt
1/3 cup and 1/4 cup unsweetened cocoa
1/2 cup milk
3 tablespoons butter, melted
1 teaspoon vanilla
1/2 cup packed brown sugar
1 3/4 cups boiling water

Preheat oven to 350 degrees. Grease a 9 inch square baking pan (I prefer glass). Combine flour, white sugar, baking powder, baking soda, salt, and 1/3 cup cocoa in a medium size bowl. Combine milk, melted butter and vanilla in a small bowl or measuring cup; stir into dry ingredients just until blended (do not over-beat). Spoon batter evenly into prepared dish. In a small bowl, combine brown sugar and 1/4 cup cocoa; sprinkle over batter in pan. Pour boiling water over entire mixture; do not stir! Bake 35 to 38 minutes. Cool 10 minutes and serve warm with whipped cream, ice cream, or half and half drizzled over the top.

"I don't remember where I got this recipe, but my English grandmother told me it is a World War II Victory recipe, made without eggs, which were in short supply in England during the war years."

Mary Makela   Fort Bragg HS, Fort Bragg, CA

Apple, Walnut, Fennel & Cheese Salad

Serves: 8   *France*

5 tablespoons extra-virgin olive oil
2 tablespoons lemon juice
1 large shallot, minced
salt, to taste
ground black pepper, to taste
3/4 cup walnuts
2 large fennel bulbs
1 red apple, quartered and cored
3 tablespoons freshly chopped Italian parsley
1 1/2 cups cheese, 3 varieties, 1/2 inch cubes

Preheat the oven to 350 degrees. In a small bowl, whisk together the olive oil, lemon juice, and shallot. Add salt and pepper to taste. Let stand for 30 minutes to allow the shallot flavor to mellow. Taste and adjust the balance as needed. Toast the walnuts on a baking sheet until fragrant and lightly colored, about 15 minutes. Let cool, then break into small pieces by hand or chop coarsely. Cut off and discard the fennel stalks, if attached. Remove the outer layer of the bulb if it is bruised or thick and fibrous. Halve the bulb and thinly slice crosswise; you can do this by hand with a sharp knife, but a vegetable slicer, such as a mandoline, makes the task easier. Cut the apple quarters crosswise into thin slices. In a large bowl, combine the fennel, apple, walnuts, parsley, and cheese. Toss with the dressing, and serve chilled.

   Nancy Ball   Arbor View HS, Las Vegas, NV

Asparagus Couscous

Serves: 4-6   *France*

2 tablespoons olive oil
2 cloves garlic
1 1/4 cups chicken broth
1 (5.6 ounce) package Near East Couscous mix-Toasted Pine Nut
10 fresh asparagus, trimmed and cut into 1/2 inch pieces
1 (6 ounce) can basil garlic tomatoes
3/4 cup Parmesan cheese, grated

In a large skillet, heat olive oil over medium heat, add garlic and cook for 2 minutes. Add broth and contents of the spice packet. Bring to a boil, add asparagus and tomatoes. Reduce heat, cover and simmer 1 minute. Stir in couscous; cover and remove from heat. Let stand for 5 minutes. Add parmesan cheese and serve.

   "An easy, delicious and nutritious dish! You can add cubed cooked chicken to make a complete meal. Not an original dish, found it on the back of a Near East box of couscous."

   Yolanda Carlos   Victor Valley HS, Victorville, CA

Basic Dessert Crepe Batter

Makes: 10-12   *France*

2 eggs
1/2 cup flour
1 tablespoon sugar
1/2 cup milk
2 tablespoons water
1/2 teaspoon melted butter

In medium mixing bowl, beat eggs. Gradually add flour and sugar alternately with milk and water, beating with electric mixer or whisk until smooth. Beat in melted butter. Cook on upside down crepe griddle or in traditional pan.

Deanna Saporetti   Lemoore HS, Lemoore, CA

Basic Quiche

Serves: 6   *France*

1 (9 inch) prepared pie crust
1 cup Swiss cheese, shredded
1/3 cup onion, fine dice
4 whole eggs
2 cups half & half
3/4 teaspoon salt
1/4 teaspoon pepper
1/8 teaspoon cayenne pepper
1 tablespoon flour
Filling Options:
1/2 cup jalapeno peppers, diced
1 cup broccoli florets
1 cup mushrooms, sliced
1 cup ham, diced
12 slices bacon, crisp
1 cup chicken, cooked
1 cup crab

Preheat oven to 425 degrees. Sprinkle grated cheese, onion and filling of choice evenly over bottom of pie crust. In a medium bowl, whisk half & half, eggs, flour and seasonings until smooth. Pour enough of the egg mixture in the pie crust to come within 1/2 inch of the top. Bake for 15 minutes; reduce heat to 300 degrees and bake for an additional 30-40 minutes longer until a knife inserted in the center comes out clean. Let stand 10 minutes; cut and serve.

Maria Nicolaides   Ocean View HS, Huntington Beach, CA

Chicken Cordon Bleu

Serves: 2   *France*

2 skinless, boneless chicken breasts
salt and pepper
2 slices cooked ham
3 slices Swiss cheese
3 tablespoons seasoned bread crumbs

Preheat oven to 350 degrees. Coat an 8 x 8 inch baking pan with cooking spray. Pound chicken breast to 1/4 inch thick. Sprinkle chicken on both sides with salt and pepper. Place 1 ham slice and 1 cheese slice on top of each piece of chicken. Roll up each chicken breast and secure with a toothpick. Sprinkle each breast with bread crumbs and place in baking dish. Bake for 35 minutes. Place 1/2 slice of cheese on top of each breast and bake for 5 more minutes. Remove toothpicks and serve.

Erna Slingland   O'Brien MS, Reno, NV

Chicken Divan Crepes
Serves: 12   *France*

1/4 cup butter
1/4 cup flour
2 cups chicken broth
2 teaspoons Worcestershire sauce
3 cups cheddar cheese, grated, divided
2 cups dairy sour cream
2 (10 ounce) packages frozen broccoli spears or 1 1/2 pounds broccoli,
    cooked and drained
2 cups cooked chicken, chopped
12 cooked crepes

Preheat oven to 350 degrees. Over medium heat, melt butter in small saucepan. Stir in flour and cook until bubbly. Add broth and Worcestershire sauce; cook, stirring until thickened. Add 2 cups cheese. Empty sour cream into medium bowl; gradually add hot cheese sauce, stirring constantly. In large shallow baking dish, place cooked broccoli and cooked chicken on each crepe. Spoon 1 tablespoon sauce over each. Fold crepe over. Pour remaining sauce over all. Sprinkle with remaining cup of cheese. Cover and heat in oven for 20-30 minutes. Makes 12 crepes.

Laurie Giauque   Olympus HS, Salt Lake City, UT

Chocolate Peanut Pillows
Serves: 10   *France*

1 (6 ounce) package semisweet chocolate pieces
1/2 cup light corn syrup
1/4 cup light cream
1 tablespoon butter
1/4 teaspoon vanilla
1/4 cup peanut butter
10 small scoops ice cream
10 cooked crepes
1/4 cup peanuts, chopped

In saucepan, melt chocolate with corn syrup at low heat, stirring until blended. Stir in cream and heat to boiling. Remove from heat; mix in butter, vanilla, and peanut butter. Place small scoop of ice cream in center of each crepe. Fold sides of crepe over ice cream, then bottom and top. Press lightly to flatten and seal. Place folded edge down on dessert plate. Spoon sauce over and sprinkle with peanuts. Makes 10 crepe pillows.

Laurie Giauque   Olympus HS, Salt Lake City, UT

Coffee Eclairs

Makes: 10-12   *France*

1/2 cup butter
1 cup boiling water
1 cup sifted flour
4 eggs
1 quart vanilla or coffee ice cream
1 cup light corn syrup
1 1/2 cups water
1 tablespoon instant coffee
3 tablespoons cornstarch
2 tablespoons butter
1 teaspoon vanilla
1/2 cup pecans, chopped

Preheat oven to 400 degrees. In a saucepan, combine the 1/2 cup butter and 1 cup boiling water and bring to a boil. Add flour all at once, stirring rapidly. Reduce heat. Cook and stir until mixture leaves sides of pan and gathers around spoon in smooth compact mass. Remove saucepan from heat. Add eggs one at a time, beat vigorously after each addition. Continue beating until eclair mixture looks satiny and breaks off when spoon is raised. Using about 1/4 cup dough for each eclair, drop dough onto ungreased baking sheet about 2 inches apart, leaving about 6 inches of space between rows. With small spatula, shape each mound into a 4 x 1 inch rectangle, rounding sides and piling dough on top. Bake until deep golden brown and puffy, about 25-30 minutes. Cool on rack. Cut each eclair in half lengthwise and remove webbing from inside. Fill bottom halves of eclairs with vanilla ice cream; replace tops. Cover and freeze. Topping: Pour corn syrup into saucepan. In separate bowl, combine the 1 1/2 cups water and instant coffee; blend in cornstarch. Stir into corn syrup. Cook and stir until sauce thickens and boils, then cook 2 minutes more. Remove from heat; add the 2 tablespoons butter and vanilla. Stir until butter melts; add chopped pecans. Serve sauce warm over frozen eclairs.

"A delicious variation on the usual custard filled eclair.
The filled eclairs freeze well so you can make them well in advance of serving."

Sue Hope   **Lompoc HS, Lompoc, CA**

Creamy French Potato Leek Soup

Serves: 6-8   *France*

4 cups potatoes
1 cup onion, diced
1 1/2 cups leeks, diced (1/4 inch dice), well rinsed
3 slices bacon
1/4 cup butter
1/4 cup flour
4 1/2 cups chicken broth (vegetable broth can be substituted)
1/4 cup half & half
salt and pepper, to taste

Clean and quarter potatoes. Use just enough water to barely cover top of potatoes. Salt water for better flavor, about 1/2 teaspoon. Cook with skin on. Boil until slightly tender. Dice or cube after they are cool. Chop leek and onion. Fry bacon; drain and chop. Melt butter in saucepan over medium-high heat. Lower heat; add onion and cook gently for about 2 minutes. Add leek and cook for an additional 6-7 minutes or until onions are soft but not brown. Add flour and stir for 2 minutes, cook without browning. (This is the roux.) Add chicken stock and bring to a boil. Dice potatoes and add with the half & half, and bacon. Simmer over medium heat until potatoes are warmed completely. Remove from heat and season to taste with salt and pepper. Garnish with cheese and crushed red pepper for some extra spice. Serve with French bread and enjoy!

"Creamy soup is on the comfort list and this fits the bill. The leeks are a sweet onion flavor that fill the room with yummy!"

Barbara Allen   Ayala HS, Chino Hills, CA

French Onion Soup
Serves: 4   *France*

1 large onion, sliced
2 tablespoons vegetable oil
2 (14 ounce) cans beef broth
1 teaspoon Worcestershire sauce
1 pinch black pepper
4 slices French bread, toasted
2/3 cup Swiss cheese, shredded

Cook and stir onion in vegetable oil in a covered large saucepan on medium heat for 20 minutes. Stir in the beef broth, Worcestershire sauce and black pepper. Heat to a boil. Remove from heat. Place toasted bread on a baking sheet and sprinkle with cheese. Broil 4-5 inches from the heat for about 1 minute or until cheese is melted and golden. Ladle soup into bowls and top with bread.

Erna Slingland   O'Brien MS, Reno, NV

Jalouises
Makes: 6   *France*

1/4 cup strawberry jelly
6 squares puff pastry
1 egg yolk
1 tablespoon milk
granulated sugar

Preheat oven to 425 degrees. Cut each puff pastry square in half. Spread jam on one side of the cut piece staying 3/4 inch away from edges. Place second strip on top of strawberry strip. Press edges with a fork so they will stick. (Looks like a skinny pop tart.) With the point of a sharp knife, make slits in the pastry at 3/8 inch intervals in center area of the pastry, cutting through only the top pastry. Beat egg yolk and add milk together. Brush on surface of pastry, making sure not to let glaze go over edges. Sprinkle or rub tops with sugar. Transfer pastry onto greased cookie sheet with metal pancake turner. Bake pastry 30 minutes. Serve warm.

Stephanie San Sebastian   Central HS, Fresno, CA

Taste OF THE WORLD

Madeline Cookies

Makes: 12   *France*

1 cup flour
1 pinch salt
2 eggs
2/3 cup sugar
1 teaspoon vanilla
zest of one lemon
10 tablespoons unsalted butter

Preheat oven to 350 degrees. Spray madeline pan with cooking spray. In a medium bowl, whisk together flour and salt. In bowl of an electric mixer with whisk attachment, beat eggs and sugar together. Add vanilla and lemon zest, then flour mixture; beat until just combined. Melt butter and add in a steady stream, mixing on low until incorporated. Spoon a rounded tablespoon of batter into each form. Bake until golden, 12-15 minutes. Cool slightly and remove from pan. Dust with powdered sugar if desired.

"This recipe was shared with my class by Mrs. M our aide. I've always wanted to make these cookies and now they are a regular cookie at our house."

Debbie Harvey   **Amador Valley HS, Pleasanton, CA**

Mama's Bread Pudding

Serves: 12   *France*

1 1/2 cups sugar, divided (1 cup and 1/2 cup)
1 teaspoon cinnamon
16 ounces 1 day old Challah bread or other egg bread, cut into 1/2 inch cubes
1/4 cup butter or margarine, melted
1/3 cup raisins
8 large eggs, lightly beaten
1 quart half and half cream
1 vanilla bean, split lengthwise or use 1-2 tsp. vanilla extract
whipped cream for topping (optional)

Heat oven to 400 degrees. Grease a 9 x 13 inch baking pan. Combine 1/2 cup sugar and cinnamon in a cup. In a large bowl, toss bread with melted butter, cinnamon/sugar mixture and raisins, then pour into the prepared pan; spread evenly. Whisk eggs, remaining 1 cup of sugar and vanilla bean to a boil in a medium saucepan, then remove vanilla bean, scrape seeds from vanilla bean (using a small spoon) and add to the egg mixture. Discard the vanilla bean shell. Gradually whisk the cream into the egg mixture. Pour over bread in baking dish. Place baking pan inside a larger roasting pan or baking dish, add enough hot water to come half way up the side of the baking dish. Bake pudding for 35-40 minutes or until custard is set and top is golden brown. Remove from oven and take the baking dish with the pudding out of the roasting pan. Serve warm or at room temperature with whipped cream if desired.

"Got this recipe from my wonderful mother-in-law. Every time I make it I have family and friends begging for me to make it again for the next holiday or get together. Enjoy!"

Jeanette Neese   **Enterprise HS, Redding, CA**

Parisian Gluten Free Crepes

Makes: about 12 crepes   *France*

3 eggs
2/3 cup gluten free flour
1 cup lowfat milk
1 tablespoon butter, divided

Blend eggs, gluten free flour and milk in blender. Place 8 inch frying pan on medium heat, add 1/4 teaspoon butter to pan and swirl to coat cooking surface of pan. When butter is bubbly, pour 2 tablespoons of crepe batter into pan and tilt pan to make desired size of crepe. If heat is correct, crepe sets at once, forming tiny bubbles. Cook crepe until edge is lightly browned and surface looks dry. Carefully lift crepe and flip over to brown lightly. Fill as desired with savory (cheese, mushrooms, ham, etc.) or sweet (fruit, jam, Nutella, whipped cream, etc.) fillings.

"Great lowfat crepe recipe even if you are not eating gluten free! Unused batter may be kept in refrigerator. Recipe courtesy of my sister and her family."

Kristine Carlin   Laguna MS, San Luis Obispo, CA

Quick Crepes

Makes: 24, 6-inch crepes   *France*

3/4 cup flour
11/2 teaspoons sugar
1/4 teaspoon baking powder
1/4 teaspoon salt
1 egg
1 cup milk
1/4 teaspoon vanilla
1 tablespoon melted butter
1 teaspoon butter to grease pan
peanut butter, granulated sugar, lemon juice, powdered sugar,
     cocoa powder, to taste

Mix together the flour, sugar, baking powder, and salt. Set aside. Beat egg, and then whisk in milk, vanilla, and melted butter. Gradually add dry ingredients to the liquid and whisk until smooth. Heat a 6 inch sauté pan over moderate heat. Lightly butter the pan with 1 teaspoon butter (if needed). Add 1 to 11/2 ounces of batter and swirl to coat pan with a thin layer of batter. Cook until edges are lightly golden. Flip and cook opposite side for about 45 seconds to 1 minute. Remove from pan and prepare with a filling before serving. On warm crepes, spread a thin layer of creamy peanut butter, and sprinkle with granulated sugar. Fold in half, and then quarters. Serve with a dusting of powdered sugar or cocoa powder. OR On warm crepes, sprinkle lemon juice and powdered sugar. Fold in half, and then quarters. Serve with a dusting of powdered sugar. Serve as described above, or rolled up with your favorite fruit and a dollop of whipped cream and a mint leaf.

"Can really be used for any course of the meal. Fill it with steamed or sautéed vegetables tossed in your favorite salad dressing for an appetizer, meat and cheese for an entree, or your choice of fruit and chocolate for a dessert."

Nancy Ball   Arbor View HS, Las Vegas, NV

Ratatouille

Serves: 6   **France**

2 tablespoons olive oil
3 cloves garlic, minced
2 teaspoons dried parsley
1 eggplant, cut into 1/2 inch cubes
salt, to taste
1 cup Parmesan cheese, grated
2 zucchini, sliced
1 large onion, sliced into rings
2 cups fresh mushrooms, sliced
1 red bell pepper, sliced
2 large tomatoes, chopped

Preheat oven to 350 degrees. Coat bottom and sides of a 1 1/2 quart casserole dish with 1 tablespoon olive oil. Heat remaining 1 tablespoon olive oil in a medium skillet over medium heat. Sauté garlic until lightly browned. Mix in parsley and eggplant. Sauté until eggplant is soft, about 10 minutes. Season with salt to taste. Spread eggplant mixture evenly across bottom of prepared casserole dish. Sprinkle with a few tablespoons of Parmesan cheese. Spread zucchini in an even layer over top. Lightly salt and sprinkle with a little more cheese. Continue layering in this fashion, with onion, mushrooms, bell pepper, and tomatoes, covering each layer with a sprinkling of salt and cheese. Bake for 45 minutes.

"I found this at allrecipes.com and used it in conjunction with the Ratatouille video and as cutting practice for my students."

Lorie Bagley   Mt. Whitney HS, Visalia, CA

Almond Kringle

Makes: 3 Coffeecakes   **Germany**

2 envelopes active dry yeast
1/2 cup sugar, divided
1/2 cup very warm water
1/2 cup milk
1 teaspoon salt
1/2 cup (1 stick) butter
2 eggs, slightly beaten
4 cups all-purpose flour
Almond Filling (recipe follows)
1 egg white beaten with 1 teaspoon water
3 tablespoons sliced blanched almonds
Filling:
1 cup almond paste (not marzipan)
1 stick softened butter
1/2 cup sugar
1/2 cup chopped preserved citron (optional)

Preheat oven to 350 degrees. Sprinkle yeast and 1 teaspoon of the sugar over very warm water. Stir to dissolve. Let stand until bubbly, about 10 minutes. Heat the milk, sugar, salt and butter just until butter melts. Cool to lukewarm. Stir in the yeast, eggs, and 2 cups of the flour and beat until smooth. Stir in enough flour to make a soft dough. Knead until elastic. Press into a greased large bowl and turn the dough over to grease. Cover and let rise in a warm place, until double in volume. Punch the dough down and divide in thirds. Roll each to 30 x 4 inches. Spread each with 1/3 of the filling and roll up, pinching the edges to seal. Be sure to pinch well so the filling won't run out while baking. Twist into a pretzel shape and place on cookie sheets covered with parchment paper. Brush with the egg white mixture and sprinkle with the almonds. Let rise until double in volume. Bake for 30 minutes. Filling: Blend the filling ingredients together and use 1/3 in each coffee cake.

"My daughter and I make several batches every year as Christmas gifts for friends. I also put a couple in the freezer for later use."

Kathleen Dickerson   Colton HS, Colton, CA

Cinnamon Wafers (ZimpftWaffeln)

Makes: 5 dozen   *Germany*

1 cup butter, softened
3/4 cup brown sugar
2 teaspoons vanilla
4 eggs
4 tablespoons cinnamon
3 1/2 cups flour

Cream butter and sugar. Add vanilla, eggs and cinnamon; stir. Add flour, 1 cup at a time; stir. Make balls (or drop by teaspoonfuls) and bake on a pizzelle iron (or on a German ZimpftWaffein iron). Cool on a wire rack. Store in an airtight container.

"This is an "old" traditional Christmas cookie from Germany."

Becky Tice   Dana Hills HS, Dana Point, CA

German Apple Banana Bread

Makes: 1 loaf   *Germany*

1 1/4 cups all-purpose flour
1/4 cup rye flour
3/4 cup white sugar
2 tablespoons dark brown sugar
1 1/4 teaspoons baking powder
1/2 teaspoon baking soda
1/2 teaspoon ground cinnamon
2 large eggs
1 cup ripe sweet bananas, mashed
1/4 cup applesauce

Preheat oven to 350 degrees. Lightly grease an 8 x 4 inch loaf pan. In a large bowl, stir together flours, sugars, baking powder, baking soda and cinnamon. Add eggs, bananas and applesauce; stir just until combined. Pour batter into prepared pan. Bake in oven for 50 to 55 minutes, until a toothpick inserted into center of loaf comes out clean. Turn out onto wire rack and allow to cool before slicing.

Lisa Marie Robey-Harris   Sonora HS, La Habra, CA

German Apple Cake

Serves: 12-16   *Germany*

2 eggs
1 cup vegetable oil
2 cups sugar
1 teaspoon vanilla
2 cups flour
2 teaspoons cinnamon
1/2 teaspoon salt
1 teaspoon baking soda
1 cup chopped walnuts
4 cups thinly sliced apples (I use granny smith)
2 (3 ounce) packages cream cheese
3 tablespoons melted butter
1 teaspoon vanilla
2 cups powdered sugar

Preheat oven to 350 degrees. Lightly grease 9 x 13 pan. In large bowl, beat by hand, 2 eggs until foamy. Add oil, sugar and vanilla and beat until creamy. Mix in flour, cinnamon, salt and baking soda. Add nuts and apples. Spread in prepared pan. Bake 40 - 60 minutes until apples are tender. Cool and frost. For frosting, beat together until creamy: cream cheese, butter, vanilla and powdered sugar.

"As a young bride I made this cake for my mother and mother-in-law for Mother's Day and it has since become a family favorite. Easy and yummy!"

Barbara Correia   **Foothill HS, Pleasanton, CA**

German Coffee Cake

Serves: About 20   *Germany*

1/2 cup soft butter
1 cup sugar
1 teaspoon vanilla
2 eggs
2 cups cake flour
1 teaspoon baking powder
1 teaspoon baking soda
1 cup sour cream
Filling:
1/2 cup sugar
1 teaspoon cinnamon
1/2 cup chopped pecans

Preheat the oven to 350 degrees. Grease a tube pan. In a large bowl, cream the butter to soften. Gradually add sugar and cream into the butter. Add vanilla and eggs and beat together until light and fluffy. In another bowl, blend together flour, baking powder, and baking soda. Add to the butter mixture alternately with the sour cream. Spread 1/2 batter into tube pan. Sprinkle 3/4 of the mixed filling over the top. Spread the rest of the batter over the filling. Sprinkle the remaining filling over the top. Place in the middle of the oven and bake about 45 minutes. Cool completely before removing from the pan.

"This recipe is from my Home Economics class at 29 Palms High School, (I am not saying what year!) from my teacher Mrs. Barnes!"

Suzi Schneider   **Bret Harte HS, Angels Camp, CA**

German Doughnuts (Greble)

Makes: 2 dozen   *Germany*

1 cup flour
1 heaping tablespoon baking powder
dash salt
1 egg
2 tablespoons oil
milk enough to moisten (about 3 tablespoons)
In a bowl, mix all ingredients together. Press dough out with fingers; about 1/4 inch thick. Cut into 2 x 3 inch pieces. With a knife make a slit all the way through the dough in the center. Heat about 2-3 inches of oil. Test to make sure oil is hot enough. Place one corner of doughnut in oil, if it sizzles, time to cook. Cook till golden brown. Drain excess oil on a plate with paper towels. In a small bowl mix 1/4 cup sugar and 1 teaspoon cinnamon. Roll doughnuts in this mixture while warm enough to coat.

Deanna Saporetti   Lemoore HS, Lemoore, CA

German Potato Salad

Serves: 12   *Germany*

10 pounds small red potatoes
1 pound bacon, cut into small pieces
1 large onion
1 teaspoon Dijon mustard
2 cups strong bouillon (use 4-6 cubes)
1/2 cup red wine vinegar
1/2 teaspoon salt
1/2 teaspoon pepper
2 teaspoons horseradish (optional)
Cook potatoes in their jackets in a covered saucepan until tender. Cut potatoes into quarters while hot. Brown the bacon in skillet. Saute the onions in the bacon skillet. Add the mustard, bouillon, vinegar, salt, pepper, and horseradish. Pour mixture over the warm potatoes and stir gently. Serve warm or chill to serve later.

"This is a recipe from my German heritage.
There is no mayo in this recipe, making it perfect for potlucks and picnics!"

Jan Tuttle   Mills HS, Millbrae, CA

Homemade German Soft Pretzels

Makes: One Dozen   *Germany*

4 teaspoons active dry yeast
1 teaspoon white sugar
1 1/4 cups warm water (110 degrees)
5 cups all-purpose flour
1/2 cup white sugar
1 1/2 teaspoons salt
1 1/2 teaspoons ground mustard
1 tablespoon vegetable oil
1/2 cup baking soda
4 cups hot water
1/4 cup kosher salt, for topping
1 cup stone ground mustard, for dipping

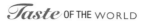

In a small bowl, dissolve yeast and 1 teaspoon sugar in warm water. Let stand until creamy, 15 minutes. In a large bowl, mix together flour, 1/2 cup sugar, ground mustard and salt. Make a well in the center; add the oil and yeast mixture. Mix and form into a dough. If the mixture is dry, add one or two tablespoons of water. Knead the dough until smooth, about 7 to 8 minutes. Lightly oil a large bowl, place the dough in the bowl and turn to coat with oil. Cover with plastic wrap and let rise in a warm place until doubled in size, about 1 hour. Preheat oven to 450 degrees. In a large bowl, dissolve baking soda in hot water. When risen, turn dough out onto a lightly floured surface and divide into 12 equal pieces. Roll each piece into a rope and twist into a pretzel shape. Once all of the dough is all shaped, dip each pretzel into the baking soda solution and place on a greased baking sheet. Sprinkle with kosher salt. Bake in preheated oven for 8-10 minutes, until browned. Serve with stone ground mustard.

Lisa Marie Robey-Harris   **Sonora HS, La Habra, CA**

Potatoes & Dumplings (Kartoffel und Glaze)

Serves: 8 -10   *Germany*

Glaze (Dumplings):
3 cups flour
3 eggs
1/2 teaspoon salt
3 tablespoons water
Kartoffel (Potatoes) and soup:
14 cups water
2 tablespoons chicken bouillon
1 tablespoon salt
11 medium potatoes, peeled and cut in half
1 onion, chopped and browned in 1 tablespoon butter
16 ounces sour cream

Make the Glaze and roll the dough into a 1 1/2 inch roll, 6 to 8 inches long. Cut into pieces approximately 1 1/4 inches long, about the size of a small finger. Bring to a boil, water, bouillon and salt. Drop glaze into the boiling water and boil for 15 to 20 minutes. Add the potatoes and continue to boil for approximately 30 minutes until done. Reduce heat below the boiling point and add the browned onion and the sour cream. Do not boil after adding sour cream! If making ahead, do not add the sour cream until ready to serve. Heat the soup just below the boiling point and stir in the sour cream.

"Recipe has been in my husband's family for over 100 years. His paternal grandmother, Mary Katherin Scheller (Schneider), brought it with her from Russia in about 1912 where German descendants worked the Volga River Valley for Catherine the Great. It's better after a night in the fridge and we like to add cooked bacon or ham."

Suzi Schneider   **Bret Harte HS, Angels Camp, CA**

Rote Grutze

Serves: 6-8   *Germany*

1 quart fruit juice (red currant, raspberry or rhubarb)
sugar to taste
6 tablespoons cornstarch
milk or cream

Bring fruit juice to slow boil. Add sugar to taste (this will depend on the sweetness of the juice and personal preference). Add small amount of water to cornstarch to make a thin paste; add slowly to boiling fruit juice. Stir constantly to keep mixture boiling slowly, about 5 minutes. Pour into glass serving bowl. Refrigerate until solidified. Serve with milk or cream as desired.

"Rote Grutze is a dessert my mother-in-law remembers being served by her grandmother and relatives when visiting Germany for a family reunion. Relatives on both sides of my husband's family came from the Schleswig-Holstein area of Germany, where this dessert is said to have its origins. My mother-in-law says she remembers it being served on top of a vanilla pudding or custard and sometimes having fruit stirred in before it was set (much as you would with a gelatin dessert)."

Laura de la Motte   Turlock HS, Turlock, CA

Soup Dumplings

Serves: 6   *Germany*

3 eggs
salt and pepper, to taste
1-1 1/2 cups flour

Mix the eggs with a fork. Add salt and pepper. Add flour until dough pulls away from the sides of the bowl. Drop by teaspoon into hot soup. Cook in soup until fluffy.

"Works best with beef soups, but can be used in any soup."

Joyce Gifford   Desert Ridge HS, Mesa, AZ

Spatzle

Serves: 4-6   *Germany*

1 2/3 cups flour
3 eggs
1/2 teaspoon sea salt (or table salt)
5 ounces water
2 tablespoons butter (To be used in a skillet to fry spatzle.)

Boil water in a medium sauce pan; bring to a rapid boil. Make a smooth, tough dough, using a wooden spoon by combining flour, eggs, sea salt and water. Put half of the dough through a Potato Ricer (use the larger holed disk) which is held over the pot of boiling water. As soon as the spatzle rise to the surface, remove them with a skimmer or slotted spoon; place them in a colander to drain. Be sure water comes to a rapid boil again. Repeat with the second half of the dough. Heat butter in a skillet and fry spatzle until golden brown on both sides. Serve immediately.

Becky Tice   Dana Hills HS, Dana Point, CA

Wassail

Serves: about 10   **England**

two oranges
whole cloves
6 cups apple cider
2 cinnamon sticks
1/4 teaspoon nutmeg
1/4 cup white Karo Syrup or honey
3 tablespoons lemon juice
1 teaspoon lemon rind
2 1/2 cups pineapple juice

Preheat oven to 350 degrees. Stick whole cloves into the rind of the uncut oranges. Place in a shallow pan with 1 cup of water and bake for 30 minutes. In a large pot, mix the remaining ingredients and simmer. Float the oranges in the pot and serve hot.

"My grandmother, Gladys Loreman, was German and she always made this Wassail for family holiday gatherings. I believe the real origin of the drink is from England."

Suzi Schneider   Bret Harte HS, Angels Camp, CA

Baklava

Makes: 3 dozen   **Greece**

1 (16 ounce) package phyllo dough
1 pound nuts, chopped
1 teaspoon ground cinnamon
1 cup butter
1 cup water
1 cup white sugar
1 teaspoon vanilla extract
1/2 cup honey

Preheat oven to 350 degrees. Butter the bottoms and sides of a 9 x 13 inch pan. Chop nuts and toss with cinnamon. Set aside. Unroll phyllo dough. Cut whole stack in half to fit pan. Cover phyllo with a dampened cloth to keep from drying out as you work. Place two sheets of dough in pan, butter thoroughly. Repeat until you have 8 sheets layered. Sprinkle 2 to 3 tablespoons of nut mixture on top. Top with two sheets of dough, butter, nuts, layering as you go. The top layer should be about 6 to 8 sheets deep. Using a sharp knife cut into diamond or square shapes all the way to the bottom of the pan. You may cut into 4 long rows then make diagonal cuts. Bake for about 50 minutes until baklava is golden and crisp. Make sauce while baklava is baking. Boil sugar and water until sugar is melted. Add vanilla and honey. Simmer for about 20 minutes. Remove baklava from oven and immediately spoon sauce over it. Let cool. Serve in cupcake papers. This freezes well. Leave it uncovered as it gets soggy if it is wrapped up.

"A Greek favorite that makes everyone think you are a master chef and is sooo easy to make! The phyllo dough for this recipe is found in the freezer section of most grocery stores. Add a little lemon zest to the sugar sauce, if desired."

Cari Sheridan   Grace Yokley MS, Ontario, CA

Greek Chicken Pita Pockets

Serves: 4-6   *Greece*

1/4 teaspoon garlic powder
1/8 teaspoon pepper
1/4 teaspoon salt
1 tablespoon lemon juice
1/4 cup mayonnaise
1/2 teaspoon cumin
1/2 teaspoon oregano
1/2 teaspoon coriander
1 cup chicken, cooked and cubed or shredded
1 tablespoon onion, minced
1 stalk celery, finely chopped
1/2 cup cheese, cubed

In a bowl, combine the first 8 ingredients. Add chicken, onion, celery and cheese. Stir together. Put in pita pockets and serve. Tastes great with a lettuce leaf as well.

Daphne Stockdale   **Carbon HS, Price, UT**

Greek Nut Pastry (Kadaifi)

Makes: 6-8   *Greece*

Filling:
1/2 cup blanched almonds
1/2 cup walnuts
2 tablespoons sugar
1/4 teaspoon cinnamon
8 ounces Kadaifi Dough (keep covered with a damp towel when not in use)
1/4 cup butter
Syrup:
1/2 cup sugar
3/4 cup water
2 teaspoons lemon juice
1 teaspoon orange-flower water or vanilla

Pastries: Preheat oven to 350 degrees. Chop nuts as finely as possible; stir together with sugar and cinnamon. Use a small amount of butter to grease round cake pan. On clean counter or large cutting board, roll the dough out to a rectangle and cut into 6-8 pieces that are more or less even. (use a sharp knife-it's still difficult) Place 1 tablespoon (use a silverware spoon) of filling on a short end of each of the pieces of dough. Roll up tightly from the short end and place in the pan, seam side down. Melt butter and pour it over the rolls. Bake 25-30 minutes or until golden and crisp. Let cool while you make the syrup. Syrup: Mix sugar, water and lemon juice in a small saucepan. Heat over medium-high heat, stirring until sugar dissolves. Boil gently about 5 minutes or until syrup thickens a bit, then turn heat off and add orange-flower water or vanilla. Pour syrup over pastry rolls and let sit for a few minutes for rolls to absorb syrup.

Julie Beers   **Sunrise Mountain HS, Las Vegas, NV**

Pastitsio

Serves: 10   Greece

Meat Mixture:
1 1/2 medium sized onions, chopped
1/4 cup butter
2 pounds lean ground beef
dash of cinnamon
salt and pepper to taste
1/2 cup water (add more as mixture cooks down)
2 tablespoons tomato paste
1 pound of macaroni, use long macaroni and break in half
3/4 cup Romano cheese, for layering, divided
Cream Sauce:
6 tablespoons butter
3/4 cup flour
1 quart of milk
3 eggs, separated

Preheat oven to 350 degrees. Sauté onion in butter until golden. Add meat and cook until well browned. Add cinnamon, salt, and pepper. Stir in water and tomato paste. Simmer 20 to 30 minutes. While the meat mixture simmers, cook macaroni according to package directions. Drain and rinse. Set aside. For the cream sauce, melt butter in a sauce pan and gradually stir in flour and cook; stirring until bubbly and well blended. Gradually stir in milk and cook until smooth and thick. Gently beat egg yolks in a small bowl and stir them into the milk mixture, taking care not to let them curdle. Now beat the egg whites and fold them into the mixture. Spoon 1/2 of the macaroni into a buttered 9 x 13 inch dish and sprinkle with 1/4 cup Romano cheese. Place all the meat mixture on top of the macaroni. Place remaining macaroni over the meat and sprinkle with another 1/4 cup of Romano cheese. Mix up the cream sauce and pour all of it over the macaroni/meat (in the dish) and sprinkle with the remaining 1/4 cup of Romano cheese. Bake uncovered for 45 minutes to 1 hour. The pastitsio should be slightly brown on top.

"A huge family favorite and is from my wonderful mother-in-law, 'Granny Madge.'"
Judy Hasperis   **Reno High School, Reno, NV**

Peloponaesian (Greek Style) Pot Roast

Serves: 6-8   Greece

2 tablespoons oil
1 2 1/2 - 3 pound pot/rump roast
8 cloves garlic
salt and pepper
3 (8 ounce) cans tomato sauce
2 tablespoons white or cider vinegar
1 teaspoon ground nutmeg
6 - 8 whole cloves
1/2 teaspoon cinnamon
1/2 teaspoon allspice
hot cooked spaghetti or other pasta

Heat the oil in a heavy pot with a lid or Dutch oven. Make slits in the roast and insert the garlic cloves. Sprinkle the roast with salt and pepper and brown the meat on all sides in the oil. Combine the rest of the ingredients except for the spaghetti and pour over the the meat. Cover, and let simmer for 1 1/2 hours or until the meat is tender. After the meat is cooked, remove the garlic cloves before slicing. Use the sauce over cooked spaghetti or other pasta.

Kathleen Dickerson   Colton HS, Colton, CA

Spanakopita
Serves: 8   *Greece*

1/2 pound feta cheese
4 ounces cream cheese
2 eggs
2 tablespoons dried parsley
1 teaspoon nutmeg
4 ounces Monterey Jack cheese
1 (10 ounce package) frozen, chopped spinach, thawed and squeezed dry
1 medium onion, chopped
2 tablespoons butter
1/2 pound phyllo pastry (about 30 sheets or layers)
12 tablespoons butter, melted

Preheat oven to 350 degrees. Blend feta cheese, cream cheese, eggs, parsley, nutmeg, and Monterey Jack cheese, a little at a time, in a blender or food processor. Combine with spinach. Sauté onion in the 2 tablespoons butter until transparent. Add to spinach mixture. Cut the phyllo sheets to fit a 9 by 12-inch baking dish. Butter the dish and place 12 layers of phyllo in it, brushing each with melted butter. Spread with cheese-spinach. Place remaining phyllo dough on top, buttering each as you layer. To make cutting easier, place the dish in the freezer for approximately 20 minutes. Cut into squares or diamonds and bake for 45 minutes or until brown and crisp. May be made ahead and reheated. It may also be frozen unbaked; thaw and bake as directed.

Tracy Shannon   Swope MS, Reno, NV

Tzatziki
Makes: 1 1/2 cups   *Greece*

2/3 cup cucumber, peeled and finely diced
1 cup plain yogurt
1 small clove garlic, minced
2 tablespoons chopped mint (about 8-10 sprigs)
1 1/2 tablespoons olive oil
1/4 teaspoon salt
pepper to taste

Combine all ingredients in a mixing bowl and stir well. Cover with plastic wrap and chill until ready to serve. Good with veggies or pita.

"One of my personal favorites, cool and refreshing. Perfect for an after school treat."

Jan Runyan   Palm Desert Charter MS, Palm Desert, CA

Corn Fritters

Serves: 12   *Holland*

2 eggs
1/2 cup milk
1 cup sifted flour
1 teaspoon baking powder
1 teaspoon salt
1 teaspoon melted butter or vegetable oil
1 cup canned whole kernel corn, drained

In a medium bowl, whisk together eggs and milk. Set aside. Sift together flour, baking powder, and salt. Mix in melted butter or oil, and make a well in the middle. Pour egg and milk batter into the dry ingredients and mix until moistened. Add corn, stir until incorporated. Drop by spoonful to deep fry until brown. (375°F) *Make sure they are cooked through, and not still doughy. Remove with a slotted spoon or tongs. Allow to drain. Serve with hot syrup, butter, or gravy.

Nancy Ball   Arbor View HS, Las Vegas, NV

Dutch Cookies

Makes: 48 cookies   *Holland*

1 pound good quality margarine or butter, softened
2 cups sugar
2 teaspoons cinnamon
1/2 teaspoon cloves
1/2 teaspoon nutmeg
1 teaspoon baking soda
1/2 cup sour cream
4 cups all-purpose flour, sifted
1/2 cup slivered almonds

Preheat oven to 325 degrees. In a large bowl, combine the margarine or butter with the sugar, cinnamon, cloves and nutmeg; mix well. In another medium bowl, combine baking soda and sour cream; blend. Add the sour cream and baking soda mixture to the margarine and sugar mixture. Mix well. Gradually add the flour to the rest of the mixture and blend well. You will need to mix the mixture with your hands as it gets thicker as you add the flour. Add the slivered almonds and mix well. Divide cookie dough in to 2 equal parts. Form each half into a roll (about 2 inches in diameter). Wrap each roll in wax paper (like a Tootsie Roll). Refrigerate overnight. Slice cookie dough into 1/4 inch slices and place on cookie sheets 2 inches apart. Bake for 15 minutes.

"This recipe is so special to our family! It came with my Grandmother from Holland where some of my Dutch relatives still reside."

Nancy Patten   Placerita JHS, Newhall, CA

Dutch Spice Cake (Ontbijtkoek)

Makes: 2 loaves   *Holland*

4 cups all-purpose flour
2 cups sugar
4 teaspoons baking powder
2 teaspoons ground cinnamon
1 1/4 teaspoons ground cloves
1 1/4 teaspoons ground nutmeg
1 teaspoon baking soda
1 teaspoon ground ginger
2 eggs
2 cups milk
1 cup honey
2 tablespoons vegetable oil

Preheat oven to 325 degrees. In large mixing bowl, combine the first eight ingredients. In a medium mixing bowl, combine the eggs, milk, honey and oil. Mix well. Stir the dry ingredients into the wet ingredients, mix until well blended. Evenly pour batter into two greased 9 x 5 x 3 inch loaf pans. Bake for 60-70 minutes, or until a toothpick inserted near the center comes out clean. Cool for 10 minutes before removing from pans to wire racks.

"This is a breakfast cake that has a sticky crust."

Astrid Curfman   Newcomb Academy, Long Beach, CA

Hungarian Goulash

Serves: 6-8   *Hungary*

4 tablespoons vegetable oil
3 or 4 medium yellow onions, diced
2 1/2 pounds stewing beef
1 tablespoon salt
1 teaspoon pepper
1 tablespoon Hungarian paprika (you can use mild or hot)
1 (14 1/2 ounce) can chicken broth
1 (8 ounce) can tomato sauce

Put oil and diced onions in a large, heavy pot and cook until the onions start to brown on the edges. Add the beef, salt, pepper and sear the meat so it's no longer red. Sprinkle the paprika on the beef. Pour in the chicken broth and tomato sauce and stir together. Cover and cook over low heat for two hours, or until the meat is very tender. Serve over cooked noodles.

"This makes a very rich and thick stew. If you aren't familiar with Hungarian paprika, be careful of the hot kind. It can be really hot!"

Kathleen Dickerson   Colton HS, Colton, CA

Brown Soda Bread

Serves: 12   *Ireland*

cooking spray
2 1/2 cups whole wheat flour
1/2 cup all-purpose flour
1/2 cup steel-cut oats
2 tablespoons brown sugar
1 tablespoon wheat germ
1 teaspoon baking soda
1 teaspoon baking powder
1/2 teaspoon salt
2 cups low-fat buttermilk
1 large egg, lightly beaten

Preheat oven to 325 degrees. Coat a 9 x 5 inch loaf pan with cooking spray. Line the pan with parchment paper and coat with cooking spray. Combine wheat flour, all-purpose flour, steel-cut oats, brown sugar, wheat germ, baking soda, baking powder and salt. Combine buttermilk and egg; add to flour mixture. Stir just until combined. Spoon the mixture into prepared pan. Bake for 1 hour and 5 minutes or until a wooden pick inserted in center comes out clean. Invert bread onto a wire rack; cool completely. Remove parchment; slice bread into 12 slices.

Mary Keane-Gruener   **Carpinteria HS, Carpinteria, CA**

Cheesy Irish Potato Soup

Serves: 5   *Ireland*

2 slices bacon, optional
2 cups chicken broth
1/4 teaspoon salt
1/4 teaspoon pepper
4 medium potatoes, cubed
3 tablespoons onion, minced
1 clove garlic, finely minced
1 cup low-fat milk
4 ounces Velvetta cheese, cubed
2 tablespoons butter
1/4 teaspoon parsley

Pan-fry 2 slices of bacon and drain on paper towel. Crumble bacon and set aside. In a 3-quart sauce pot, bring to boil, chicken broth, salt and pepper. Add cubed potatoes, onion and garlic. Return to boil, then reduce heat to simmer for 15 minutes or until potatoes are soft. Remove from heat and mash potato mixture, but do not drain excess water. Return to low-heat and whisk in milk, cheese and parsley. Serve immediately and top with crumbled bacon. Enjoy!

"You don't have to be Irish to love this soup! It is quick and easy to prepare, inexpensive, and best of all delicious!"

Joan Schlesinger   **Hart HS, Newhall, CA**

Ground Beef, Corn and Potatoes

Serves: 6   **Ireland**

5-6 medium potatoes
1/4 cup margarine or butter
1/4 cup milk
1/4 teaspoon salt
1/4 teaspoon pepper
1 pound ground beef
1 medium onion, chopped
1/4 teaspoon salt
1/4 teaspoon pepper
1 (15 ounce) can creamed corn
3 tablespoons margarine or butter

Preheat oven to 350 degrees. Peel and cut potatoes into 1 inch cubes. Boil in a large pot of water until tender. Drain liquid and place potatoes in a large bowl. With an electric mixer, mash potatoes. Add margarine and mix, allow margarine to melt in hot potatoes. Add milk, salt and pepper, and mix until creamy smooth (add more milk if needed). Season to taste. Fry ground beef with salt, pepper and onion in a Dutch Oven until browned. Drain fat from beef. Open the can of creamed corn and spread over top of the ground beef. Spread mashed potatoes on top and cover the corn and beef completely. Drop small dots of margarine or butter on top. Place a lid on the Dutch oven and place in the oven for 20 minutes. Remove from oven and serve.

"This is an old family comfort food. Great for cold winter days."

Doris Fossen   **Sierra Vista JHS, Canyon Country, CA**

Irish Soda Bread

Makes: 1 round loaf   **Ireland**

2 cups white flour
2 teaspoons baking soda
2 teaspoons baking powder
1/2 teaspoon table salt
3 tablespoons sugar
3 tablespoons butter, softened
1 cup buttermilk
1/2 cup raisins
2 tablespoons caraway seeds, optional
Confectioner's or granulated sugar

Preheat oven to 375 degrees. In a large bowl, mix the flour, baking soda, baking powder, salt and sugar. Using a pastry blender, cut the butter into the dry mixture until it consists of uniform coarse crumbs. Add the buttermilk, raisins and caraway seeds. Mix until barely moistened. Do not over mix. Gather into a ball and knead for 1 minute on a lightly floured surface. Roll into a ball and pat down to form a slightly flat loaf. Using a floured, sharp knife, cut a large cross, 1 1/2 inches deep, into the dough. Sprinkle the top with sugar and bake on an ungreased cookie sheet for 35 minutes.

"Adults like the caraway seeds but the younger folk prefer it without. Great with tea."

Lisa Burson   **San Luis Obispo HS, San Luis Obispo, CA**

St. Patrick's Day Scones

Serves: 4   *Ireland*

3/4 cup flour, sifted
1 1/2 teaspoons baking powder
1/4 teaspoon salt
1 tablespoon sugar
2 tablespoons plus 2 teaspoons shortening
1/4 cup quick cooking oats
1/3 cup milk
1/2 teaspoon melted butter
cinnamon and sugar, to taste

Preheat oven to 450 degrees. Sift flour, baking powder, salt and sugar into mixing bowl. Cut in shortening. Add oats and milk; stir just until blended. Form dough into a ball. Divide dough into 2 parts; press each part into a circle. Spread each circle with melted butter; sprinkle with cinnamon and sugar mixture. Arrange on cookie sheet. Bake for 12-15 minutes or until nicely browned.

"Always a class favorite."

Joy Aiello   **Porterville HS, Porterville, CA**

Artichoke Parmesan Soup

Serves: 4-5   *Italy*

2 tablespoons butter
1/4 medium onion, finely chopped
1/4 cup carrots, finely chopped
1/2 celery stalk, finely chopped
1 teaspoon thyme leaves
3/8 teaspoon salt
1/8 teaspoon pepper
3/4 teaspoon granulated garlic
1/3 cup flour
2 cups chicken stock
1 cup half and half
1 (15 ounce) can artichoke hearts, drained and chopped
1/2 cup grated Parmesan cheese

Melt butter in a 3-quart saucepan; add and cook onions, carrots, celery, thyme, salt, pepper and garlic until tender. Add flour to vegetable and seasoning mixture. With a whisk stir to make a roux. Mixture will be slightly doughy. Add chicken stock and bring to a boil, stirring constantly. Stock should thicken quickly. Stir in half and half and reduce to simmer. Add artichokes; heat through. Add cheese and whisk until a smooth consistency forms. Serve hot with slices of Artisan bread.

"An instant favorite of students serious about culinary arts as a career."

Anne Hawes   **Cottonwood HS, Murray, UT**

Aunt Nano's Ricotta Cake

Makes: 9 x 13 cake   *Italy*

2 pounds Ricotta Cheese (don't use Fat Free but Lite is okay)
3/4 cup sugar
3 eggs
1 Lemon flavor package cake mix, with pudding (plus eggs, oil and water
  according to cake mix package instructions)

Preheat oven to 350 degrees. Grease and flour 9 x 13 inch cake pan. Prepare cake mix per package instructions and pour into prepared cake pan. In a medium bowl, stir together ricotta cheese, sugar and eggs. Spoon the cheese mixture gently over the cake batter. Gently spread. Do not mix cheese mixture and cake batter. Bake for 60-65 minutes. Cool at least 2 hours. Invert to serve. Keep chilled.

"Aunt Nano made this cake for many nieces and nephews. It is a family favorite that has been passed on to the next generation."

Mary Jo Cali   **Arroyo Grande HS, Arroyo Grande, CA**

Baked Ziti

Serves: 10   *Italy*

1 pound dry ziti pasta
2 (26 ounce) jars spaghetti sauce
6 ounces provolone cheese, sliced
1 1/2 cups sour cream
6 ounces mozzarella cheese
2 tablespoons Parmesan cheese, grated
Optional: ricotta to your liking

Preheat the oven to 350 degrees. Cook pasta according to package directions. Butter a 9 x 13 baking dish. Layer as follows: 1/2 ziti, provolone cheese, sour cream, 1/2 sauce mixture, remaining ziti, mozzarella cheese and remaining sauce mixture. Top with grated Parmesan cheese. Bake for 30 minutes in the preheated oven, or until cheeses are melted.

"Very economical and tasty."

Dawn Maceyka   **Great Oak HS, Temecula, CA**

Best Garlic Bread

Serves: 6-8   *Italy*

1/2 cup butter, softened
1/2 teaspoon garlic powder
1 teaspoon parsley
2 tablespoons Parmesan cheese
dash cayenne pepper
dash paprika
1/4 teaspoon salt
1 loaf French bread

Mix everything except bread together. Slice loaf of bread in half and spread mixture on. Broil on high for about 5 minutes or until top is lightly browned. Be sure to watch it so it doesn't burn!

Theona Blanchard   **Centennial HS, Las Vegas, NV**

Calzone with Chard, Sun-Dried Tomatoes & Four Cheeses

Serves: 4-6   *Italy*

2 cloves garlic, minced
1 bunch Swiss chard leaves (remove center rib), cooked, well drained, chopped
1/4 cup basil leaves, chopped
2 tablespoons fresh parsley, minced
salt
freshly ground black pepper
freshly ground nutmeg
1 cup provolone or Italian Fontina cheese
1 cup mozzarella cheese, grated
1/3 cup Gorgonzola cheese or goat cheese
1/2 cup Parmesan cheese
1/2 cup sun-dried tomatoes, drained and diced
olive oil
homemade pizza dough or 1 (13.8 ounce) can refrigerated pizza crust

Toss garlic, Swiss chard, herbs, seasonings, cheeses, and sun-dried tomatoes in a medium bowl and season to taste. Punch dough down and divide into 2 to 4 portions. Roll out on lightly floured surface and mound filling on one side of the circle you have created. Fold your circle of dough over top edge; pinch or crimp together to seal. Brush with olive oil. Repeat with other portions. Transfer to a lightly greased baking sheet keeping dough a few inches apart. With a sharp knife, make several slits in the top. Bake in the lower third of the oven 15 to 20 minutes or until well browned. Remove from the oven. Brush with olive oil and sprinkle with freshly grated Parmesan cheese. Allow the calzone to stand 15 minutes or longer before serving. Serve warm or at room temperature.

"Culinary Arts Class, Santa Monica Junior College, 1994, Carolyn Thacker, instructor. Use homemade or pre-made pizza dough; filling is easy, taste is incredible."

Maria Scirone, M.A.   **Westlake HS, Westlake, CA**

Cheese Manicotti

Serves: 6   *Italy*

6 manicotti shells
1/2 teaspoon salt
1 teaspoon olive oil
water
1/3 medium zucchini, grated
4-6 large spinach leaves, washed, dried and finely chopped
2 tablespoons yellow or green onion, chopped
1 cup assorted cheese (ricotta, mozzarella, Parmesan, Monterey)
1 egg
1/4 teaspoon nutmeg
1/4 teaspoon pepper
1/4 teaspoon paprika
1/8 teaspoon salt
2 tablespoons fresh or dried parsley, chopped
1 1/2 cups marinara/spaghetti sauce, divided

Fill a large saucepan 2/3 full with water. Add salt and olive oil. Bring to a boil. Lower heat to a gentle boil and carefully lower manicotti shells into water. Simmer on a low boil for 2-3 minutes until pasta is pliable, but still undercooked. Using a slotted spoon, remove each shell to a plate to cool. Grate zucchini onto a paper towel. Squeeze zucchini with paper towel to remove excess moisture. Tightly roll spinach leaves together. Slice into very thin strips. Chop onion. Mix zucchini, spinach, and onion together in large bowl. Add cheese, egg, and seasonings to zucchini mixture. Mix well. Line bottom of 8 x 8 baking pan (preferably glass) with 1 cup marinara. Carefully use a dinner knife to insert/slide filling into each shell. Carefully set filled shells onto sauce; keep top of shells clean of sauce. Spoon remaining 1/2 cup sauce across the center only of the shells, leaving the ends of the shells clean. Cover with plastic wrap and refrigerate. Keeps for up to two days in refrigerator. OR: cover with foil and bake at 350 degrees for 20 minutes. Garnish with freshly grated Parmesan and chopped fresh basil.

"An original popular favorite with family, friends, and students. Accompany with a green vegetable, salad, and crusty French bread for a perfect meal."

Christine Becker   Paradise HS, Paradise, CA

Chicken & Spinach Calzone

Serves: 4   *Italy*

Crust:
1/2 cup warm water (110 degrees)
1/4 teaspoon sugar
3/4 teaspoon active dry yeast
1 1/4 cups all-purpose flour
1/8 teaspoon salt
1 teaspoon olive oil
2 teaspoons basil
1 teaspoon cornmeal (for sprinkling on pan)
Filling:
6 ounces chicken breast
1 1/4 teaspoons oregano
1 1/4 teaspoons rosemary
1/4 teaspoon salt
1 Roma tomato, sliced or diced
3 ounces frozen spinach, defrosted and patted dry
6 ounces mozzarella cheese
2 tablespoons Parmesan cheese
Marinara sauce for dipping

Crust: Mix sugar into the warm water. Sprinkle yeast on top. Wait for 10 minutes or until it gets all foamy. In a large mixing bowl, put flour, salt and olive oil. Add water mixture. Combine. Using hook attachment, knead with mixer for 5-6 minutes until you have a moderately stiff dough that is smooth and elastic (add a bit more flour if you need to). Fold in basil. *Filling:* Preheat oven to 375 degrees. Cut chicken into bite sized pieces and season with spices. Sauté chicken in a skillet with oil until just cooked through. Do not overcook. Prepare spinach and slice tomatoes. Roll out dough. Add fillings to one side of dough. Fold in half. Pinch edges closed. Brush melted butter and sprinkle with Parmesan cheese. Bake on well greased cookie sheet for 15 minutes.

Lori Fuxa   Rancho Alamitos HS, Garden Grove, CA

Crispy Wisconsin Mascarpone Rigatoni

Serves: 12 (5 pieces per serving)   *Italy*

1/2 cup (4 ounces) Wisconsin Crave Brothers Mascarpone
1 1/2 cup (12 ounces) Wisconsin Ricotta Cheese
1 cup (about 3 ounces) Wisconsin Romano Cheese, finely grated
2 tablespoons fresh mint leaves, finely chopped
1/2 teaspoon cocoa powder
3 eggs
2 tablespoons water
1 pound rigatoni pasta, cooked al dente
2 cups fine breadcrumbs
Olive oil for frying
2 cups marinara sauce
Fresh basil leaves, finely chopped
1/2 pound Wisconsin Provolone Cheese, shaved

In medium mixing bowl, whisk together the Mascarpone, Ricotta, Romano, mint and cocoa. Refrigerate for one hour. Preheat oven to 400ºF. In medium bowl, beat eggs and water together. Dip rigatoni in egg mixture and roll in breadcrumbs; being sure to coat ends well. Pour 1/4 inch olive oil in bottom of large sauté pan. Heat oil over medium heat. Fry rigatoni until crisp on each side, about 1 minute. Remove and drain on paper towels. Pipe refrigerated cheese filling into fried rigatoni and place in baking pan; bake for 5 minutes. Meanwhile, heat marinara sauce. Place a dollop of sauce on small plate and place 5 stuffed rigatoni on top at various angles. Garnish with fresh basil. Sprinkle with shaved Provolone cheese.

Wisconsin Milk Marketing Board   **WisDairy.com**

Easy Black Bean Lasagna

Serves: 8   *Italy*

1 15-ounce can black beans,
  rinsed and drained
1 28-ounce can crushed tomatoes,
  undrained
1 15-ounce can fat-free refried beans
3/4 cup onion, chopped
1/2 cup green bell pepper, chopped
3/4 cup chunky-style salsa
1 teaspoon chili powder

1/2 teaspoon cumin
8 ounces Cottage Cheese
1/8 teaspoon garlic powder
  (or 1 tsp. fresh garlic)
2 eggs
Salt and pepper to taste
10 lasagna noodles, uncooked
1-1/2 cups each Wisconsin Cheddar
  and Mozzarella cheese, shredded

Heat oven to 350°F. Spray a 9 x 13 baking dish with cooking spray. In a large bowl, combine black beans, tomatoes, refried beans, onion, green pepper, salsa, chili powder and cumin. Mix well. In a small bowl, combine Cottage cheese, garlic powder, eggs and salt and pepper. Spread 1 cup of the tomato mixture in bottom of baking dish. Top with half of the noodles, overlapping slightly. Top with half of remaining tomato mixture. Spoon Cottage cheese mixture over the top, and top with half of the cheese, then the remaining noodles, tomato mixture and cheese. Cover with spray-coated foil (can be refrigerated up to one day). Bake at 350°F for 45 minutes, uncover and let stand 15 minutes before serving. (If refrigerated beforehand, add 15 minutes to baking time.)

Wisconsin Milk Marketing Board   **WisDairy.com**

Crispy Wisconsin
Mascarpone Rigatoni

Easy Black Bean Lasagna

Italian Sausage with Pasta and Herbs

Sweet and Spicy Thai Pork Loin

Italian Sausage with Pasta and Herbs

Serves: 4-6   *Italy*

1 pound Italian dinner sausage
1 tablespoon olive oil
2 cups zucchini, cubed
1/2 red bell pepper, diced
8 ounces rotini pasta
1 cup ricotta cheese, part skim
2 tablespoons dried herbs, (basil, sage, parsely)
Parmesan cheese, freshly grated

Cut sausage diagonally into 1-inch pieces and cook sausage in a large skillet over medium heat, turning to cook and brown evenly, about 10 to 15 minutes or until internal temperature reaches 160 degrees F. Set aside. Cool slightly and cut diagonally into 1-inch pieces. Heat olive oil in a large skillet and add zucchini and red pepper. Cook over medium heat until tender but still crisp, about 3-4 minutes. Cook the rotini according to the directions on the package. Drain and reserve 1 cup cooking water. Add pasta to skillet and stir in ricotta. Add 1/2 cup pasta water and stir until creamy. Stir in sausage. Add more water if mixture is too dry. Sprinkle with fresh herbs and Parmesan cheese.

National Pork Board   PorkBeInspired.com

Sweet and Spicy Thai Pork Loin

Serves: 8   *Thailand*

2 pounds Pork Loin, cut into 1-inch cubes, trimmed
1 yellow onion, chopped
1 red bell pepper, chopped
1 cup long, thin beans, OR string beans, cut into 1-inch lengths
1 cup Sweet Thai chile sauce, (like May Ploy or Thai Kitchen)
1/2 cup chicken broth, reduced-sodium
1/2 teaspoon salt
1/4 cup water
1 tablespoon basil leaves, torn
1 tablespoon mint leaves, torn
1 tablespoon cilantro leaves , torn

Combine all ingredients except fresh herbs and cook at low for 4 to 5 hours (or on high for 2 to 2 1/2 hours). Just before serving, add fresh herbs and check seasoning. Transfer pork and sauce to a serving bowl. Serve over rice or Asian noodles.

National Pork Board   PorkBeInspired.com

Chicken Piccatta

Serves: 2   *Italy*

4 chicken cutlets
2 tablespoons vegetable oil
1/4 cup of chicken broth or dry white wine
1 teaspoon garlic, minced
1/2 cup chicken broth
2 tablespoons lemon juice
1 tablespoon capers
2 tablespoons butter
fresh lemon slices
fresh parsley, chopped for garnish

Season cutlets with salt and pepper. Dust chicken with flour. Spray pan with nonstick cooking spray and add vegetable oil. Heat pan for about 2-3 minutes. Sauté cutlets 2-3 minutes on each side. Transfer cutlets to a warm plate. Pour off any extra fat from pan. Deglaze pan with the 1/4 cup of wine or broth and add garlic. Cook until garlic is slightly brown and liquid is nearly gone, about 2 minutes. Add the broth, lemon juice, and capers. Return cutlets back to pan for about 1 minute. Remove cutlets once again. Finish sauce with the butter and lemon slices. Pour sauce over cutlets once butter melts. Garnish with the parsley.

"Easy and elegant dish."

Jennell Acker   **Chino Hills HS, Chino Hills, CA**

Chocolate Chip Biscotti

Serves: 8   *Italy*

3 eggs
1 cup oil (I use 1/2 cup extra light olive oil and 1/2 cup amaretto)
1 cup sugar (can use + 1/4 cup)
3 cups flour (I use more like 3 1/2 cups with 2 cups whole wheat flour)
1 tablespoon baking powder
1/4 teaspoon salt
1 cup chocolate chips

Preheat oven to 375 degrees. Mix eggs, oil, and sugar. Add flour, baking powder, salt and chocolate chips to mixture until blended. Form dough into 3 logs. Bake for 17 minutes. Take them out of the oven. Slice the logs into 1/2 inch wide slices. Lay the slices cut side down on the baking sheet and sprinkle with cinnamon and sugar. Bake them again 5 minutes (or longer for harder). Kids and adults love these! They don't come out too hard, so you can eat them like a regular cookie.

"My sister Sue's signature recipe."

Julie Carriere   **North Monterey County HS, Castroville, CA**

Chopped Italian Salad

Serves: 4 *Italy*

Salad Ingredients:
1 head Romaine lettuce, cut into 1 inch squares
1/4 pound salami or pepperoni, sliced into strips
1/3 cup red onion, sliced very thin
1/4 cup artichoke hearts, drained, rinsed and chopped
1/2 cup green olives, pitted and rough chopped
Dressing Ingredients:
3 tablespoons red wine vinegar
1/4 cup olive oil
1/2 teaspoon salt
1/4 teaspoon fresh ground black pepper
1/2 cup fresh parmesan, grated

In a large glass or stainless steel bowl, combine the romaine, salami, onions, artichoke hearts, and olives. Toss to combine. Combine the dressing ingredients and pour them over the salad. Toss thoroughly to combine the ingredients.

"This salad is quick and full of flavor. The perfect starter for any Italian meal!"

Carissa McCrory Whitney HS, Rocklin, CA

Easy Calzone

Makes: 4 individual servings *Italy*

1/2 pound ground beef
1/2 onion, chopped
1/2 cup tomato sauce
1/4 teaspoon pepper
1/2 teaspoon salt
pinch oregano
1/4 teaspoon garlic powder
1/3 pound Jack cheese, grated
Optional: olives, bell pepper, pepperoni, or other favorite pizza toppings
1 loaf Bridgeford frozen bread dough, thawed

Preheat oven to 375 degrees. Brown ground beef, add chopped onion. Add tomato sauce, salt, pepper, garlic powder, and oregano. Simmer for about 10 minutes. If you have optional ingredients, add them now. Divide thawed bread dough into 4 equal pieces. Using a rolling pin, roll each piece of dough into a circle. Evenly divide the meat mixture onto the dough rounds and evenly add the grated cheese. Fold the circles in half to form a half circle, pinch the edges together to seal. Place onto a greased cookie sheet and bake for 20-25 minutes or until golden brown. *To make your life even easier, use marinara sauce or pizza sauce instead of the tomato sauce, pepper, salt, oregano, and garlic powder. Serve hot! I like the marinara sauce poured over the calzone as well, topped with a little grated cheese.

"This is easy and can be prepared ahead of time and baked when needed. Easy and fun for the pizza lovers!"

Elizabeth Thornburg Selma HS, Selma, CA

Eggplant Ragu
Serves: 8-10   *Italy*

6 cups eggplant, skin on, cut into cubes
1 large onion, bite sized cubes
1 cup red bell pepper, bite sized cubes
1 cup green bell pepper, bite sized cubes
1 cup mushrooms, cut into quarters
5 cloves garlic, minced
1 (29 ounce) can tomato sauce
2 teaspoons oregano
1 teaspoon garlic salt
1 teaspoon celery salt
1/2 teaspoon black pepper
1/3 cup olive oil

Wipe off the mushrooms with a damp paper towel; slice into quarters. Cut the eggplant into cubes leaving skin on. Place on paper toweling.Heat the olive oil on a medium flame. Sauté the onions, peppers and eggplant in the olive oil for 5 minutes. Add the mushrooms and garlic and continue sautéing for 5 more minutes. Add the tomato sauce and seasonings and stir. Reduce heat to a low flame and simmer for 30-45 minutes until all of the vegetables are tender. Serve over rice, pasta, or polenta.

Maria Nicolaides   Ocean View HS, Huntington Beach, CA

Fusilli Pasta with Almond-Cream Pesto
Serves: 6   *Italy*

Salad:
1 pound fusilli pasta
4 cups small broccoli florets
1 cup carrots, 1/4 inch diced
1 red bell pepper, seeded, deribbed, and cut into long slivers
1 cup fresh or frozen corn kernels
1 cup slivered snow peas
3 tablespoons olive oil
Pesto:
2/3 cup chopped almonds, pan-toasted until lightly golden
1/2 cup fresh basil leaves
1/2 cup cilantro leaves
1 jalapeno chile, seeded and chopped
1 cup milk
1/3 cup ricotta cheese
salt
freshly ground pepper

Cook pasta in a large pot of boiling water al dente. After 5 minutes of cooking time, add the broccoli and carrot. After 8 minutes, add the bell pepper and corn. Add the snow peas in the last 30 seconds of cooking. Ladle out 1/2 cup cooking liquid and set aside. Remove the pan from the heat and drain the pasta and vegetables. Transfer to a bowl, and, while warm, toss with olive oil. To make the pesto: grind the almonds in a food processor. Add the remaining ingredients and reserved cooking liquid and process until smooth. Pour the pesto over the hot pasta and toss to mix. Season with salt and pepper. Serve warm or at room temperature.

"Any pasta that will hold the sauce will do well."

Cherri Farrell   **College Park HS, Pleasant Hill, CA**

Garbanzo Salad

Serves: 6-8   *Italy*

2 (15 ounce) cans garbanzo beans
1/4 cup celery, diced
2 tablespoons parsley, minced
1/4 cup green onion, minced
1/4 cup vinegar
1/2 cup olive oil
1 clove garlic, crushed
1/4 teaspoon paprika
1/2 teaspoon salt
1/2 teaspoon oregano

Drain and rinse garbanzo beans, then drain thoroughly. Combine beans, celery, parsley and green onions. Beat together vinegar, oil, garlic, paprika, salt and oregano, then pour over bean mixture. Toss to mix well and chill several hours or overnight. Can be served on a lettuce leaf and/or garnished with green pepper rings.

"This is always a great salad for a pot luck or barbecue."

Cheri Schuette   **Valley View MS, Simi Valley, CA**

Garlic Cheese Bread

Serves: 4   *Italy*

1 loaf French bread or baguette (sliced lengthwise down the middle)
3/4 cup butter, room temperature
1 teaspoon garlic, finely minced
2 teaspoons minced Italian parsley
3 tablespoons cheddar cheese, grated
3 tablespoons Parmesan or similar cheese, grated

Preheat oven to high broil. Combine the softened butter, garlic, parsley, and cheeses in a small bowl. Evenly spread the mixture over the bread. Broil until the bread is beginning to brown and the cheese mixture is bubbling. Slice and serve.

"This is Sarah Delevati's (my grandmother) recipe. Born in Palermo, Italy and moved to Martinez, California where she spent the majority of her life. My class has used it for catering lunches and our "family" meals. Mangia!"

Jackie Lawson   **Dublin HS, Dublin, CA**

Gnocchi

Serves: 3-4   *Italy*

1 potato per person
flour, approximately one cup of flour to 3 medium potatoes

Boil potato until you can pierce center with fork with no resistance. Set cooked potato on pan to cool. Just cool enough to handle. Peel potato, while still warm. (hold potato with a towel/napkin, etc.) Best to peel while still warm. Cut into chunks. Rice potato onto a cookie sheet.(using a ricer tool). Potato should still be warm at this point. Let potato come to room temperature. If they are warm to the touch, it's too soon. Pour riced potato onto floured surface. Start with a cup of flour. Remember, you can always add, you can't take away. You can pour the whole cup on the board, but add slowly. The size of potato, the moisture in the air, etc. can make a difference. Mix until a solid ball forms. Maybe 3-5 minutes. Cut into pieces, roll into logs. Cut into bite size "nuggets". About an inch/nuckle size. Press finger in center of each piece and roll towards you. Place on lightly floured cookie sheet. Cover with towel. Cook soon, don't let sit for a long period. Or, freeze. Place single layer on pan, place pan in freezer. When frozen transfer to ziplock bag. Boil water, add salt, cook until they float. Remove from water and cover with spaghetti sauce. Enjoy!

"From my Aunt Theresa Maragoni through my cousin Darlene. My aunt never added salt or eggs, but if you ever add too much flour, add an egg. She would not have added water. The recipe comes from her childhood in Italy, the way her mom taught her. It is very basic due to the lack of items, due to the war."

Ruth Schletewitz   **Rafer Johnson JHS, Kingsburg, CA**

Grandma Bettensoli Silveira Spaghetti Sauce

Serves: 8-12   *Italy*

3-4 tablespoons olive oil
2 yellow onions, finely chopped
box of sliced mushrooms
4 cloves garlic, minced
3 links mild Italian sausage
3 links hot Italian sausage
1 pound ground beef
2 (28 ounce) cans tomato puree
2 (6 ounce) cans tomato paste
2 (14.5 ounce) chicken broth
1 teaspoon chicken granules
2 teaspoons sugar
2-3 tablespoons of oregano or basil.
season to taste with salt, pepper, onion powder and garlic powder

In large stock pot, add olive oil and sauté first three ingredients until tender. Remove sausage from casings and add to pot. Add hamburger and cook until meat is done, stirring to break up meat into small pieces. Drain grease if necessary. Add the rest of the ingredients and simmer for a couple of hours. Add pepper flakes if a spicy sauce is preferred.

"Grandma Elsie is famous for her sauce! The surprise ingredient is chicken broth! Makes a large quantity and is easy to freeze in small containers and use when needed."

Anne Silveira   **Shasta High HS, Redding, CA**

Healthy Italian Meat Loaf

Serves: 8 to 10   *Italy*

2 pounds ground turkey
1 medium white onion, chopped
5 cloves garlic, minced
3 cups fresh whole wheat bread crumbs
1 cup fresh Italian parsley, chopped
2 tablespoons Italian seasonings
salt and freshly ground black pepper, to taste
2 eggs, lightly beaten
1/2 cup ketchup
1/2 cup dry red wine
2 cups fresh basil leaves
4 ounces sun-dried tomatoes (packed in oil), drained
1 pound mozzarella cheese, thinly sliced

Preheat oven to 375 degrees. Combine ground turkey, onion, garlic, bread crumbs, parsley, Italian seasonings, and salt and pepper to taste in a large bowl. Mix well. Add the eggs, ketchup and wine and mix thoroughly. Lay out 1 large sheet of waxed paper or parchment paper. Spread the meat loaf mixture out in a 15 x 12-inch rectangle on the waxed paper. Arrange the basil leaves over the surface. Scatter the sun-dried tomatoes over the basil leaves and arrange three-fourths of the mozzarella cheese on top. Using the wax paper as an aid and starting from one short side, roll up the meat like a jelly roll. Peel back the paper as you roll. Place seam side down on a baking sheet lined with aluminum foil. Bake 1 hour. Place the remaining mozzarella cheese over the top of the loaf and bake until the cheese is melted and bubbling; about 10 minutes more.

"A hot or cold crowd pleaser, and healthy. Try 1 pound turkey sausage and 1 pound ground turkey instead of 2 pounds of ground turkey. You are going to enjoy this recipe!"

Brenda Burke   **Mt. Whitney HS, Visalia, CA**

Italian Cheese Rustica Pie

Serves: 6-8   *Italy*

1 package All-Ready Pie Crust
1 tablespoon flour
3 eggs
1 cup (4 ounces) shredded mozzarella cheese
1 cup (4 ounces) cubed Swiss cheese
1 cup cooked ham, cubed
1 cup ricotta cheese
4 tablespoons grated Parmesan cheese, divided
1/2 teaspoon parsley flakes
1/4 teaspoon oregano leaves

Preheat oven to 375 degrees. Prepare pie crust according to package instructions for two crust pie, using a deep 9 inch pie pan. In a large bowl, slightly beat 3 eggs. Add mozzarella cheese, Swiss cheese, ham, ricotta and 3 tablespoons of Parmesan cheese. Mix well. Spoon egg mixture into pie crust lined pan. Top with second pie crust. Flute edges and cut 4, 1 inch slits in top. Brush a beaten egg over the pie crust and sprinkle with remaining tablespoon of Parmesan cheese. Bake for 50-60 minutes. Let stand for 10 minutes before cutting.

"My sister has made this dish for years, typically as a gift of love when a home cooked meal is most welcome."

Mary Jo Cali　　　　　　　　　**Arroyo Grande HS, Arroyo Grande, CA**

Italian Cookie Slices

Makes: 5 1/2 Dozen　　　　　　　　　　　　　　　*Italy*

1/2 cup butter
1 cup sugar
3 large eggs
1 1/2 teaspoons anise flavoring
3 cups flour
1 teaspoon salt
1 tablespoon baking powder
1 cup ground walnuts or blanched almonds

Preheat oven to 350 degrees. Sift dry ingredients together and set aside. Cream together butter, sugar and anise flavoring. Beat eggs, one at a time into sugar mixture. Add flour mixture and mix. Add ground nuts. Stir until firm. (If it is too soft, add a bit more flour.) Make two loaves about 1" thick on a cookie sheet. Bake until firm to touch, 30-35 minutes. Remove and cool slightly. While warm, slice into thin slices and return to oven to dry for 10-20 minutes. Store in airtight container.

"Sort of a take on a biscotti cookie. It is not too sweet and makes a nice pairing with coffee, tea or wine. My mom who is 92 still makes these cookies for us!"

Maria Fregulia　　　　　　　　　**Lassen HS, Susanville, CA**

Italian Tortellini soup

Serves: 6　　　　　　　　　　　　　　　　　*Italy*

1 pound Italian sausage or Jimmy Dean mild sausage
2 cloves garlic, minced
1 small onion, diced
3-4 cups chicken broth
1 cup white wine
1 (16 ounce) can Italian stewed tomatoes, chopped and juice
1 (16 ounce) can tomato sauce
1 (16 ounce) package baby carrots
1 teaspoon basil leaves, dried
1/2 teaspoon oregano
2 tablespoons parsley
2 medium zucchini
1 (8 ounce) package tortellini (your choice of flavor)

In a soup pot, brown and cook sausage, garlic and onion. Add rest of ingredients except zucchini, tortellini and parsley. Simmer for 30 minutes. Stir in zucchini, tortellini and parsley. Simmer another 30 minutes. Add more broth if it needs to be thinner.

"I use my slow cooker. Brown the sausage, garlic and onion first. Then add everything to the slow cooker except the tortellini and cook slow all day. Add the tortellini an hour before serving. Enjoy!"

Gail McAuley　　　　　　　　　**Lincoln HS, Stockton, CA**

Italian Wedding Soup

Serves: 4-6 *Italy*

Meatballs:
1/2 pounds extra lean ground beef
1 egg, lightly beaten
2 tablespoons bread crumbs
1 tablespoon Parmesan cheese, grated
1/2 teaspoon fresh basil, chopped
1/2 teaspoon onion powder
1/2 teaspoon garlic powder
pinch salt and pepper
Soup:
6 cups chicken broth
1 tablespoon olive oil
3 cups fresh spinach and/or escarole OR 1 cup frozen spinach
1 teaspoon fresh basil, chopped
3/4 cup Orzo, uncooked
1 teaspoon garlic, finely chopped
1/2 cup carrot, finely chopped
1/2 cup celery, finely chopped

Preheat oven to 250 degrees. Mix meatball ingredients together by hand. Shape into tiny meatballs. Bake for 45 minutes (or pan fry in olive oil for crispier exterior). In saucepan, heat broth to a boil. Stir in cooked meatballs and remaining ingredients. Return to boil. Reduce heat to medium. Cook at a slow boil 10 minutes or until Orzo is tender, stirring frequently. Serve sprinkled with cheese. Note: To make this a quick recipe, you can use frozen meatballs from the market. If they are too large, follow cooking directions and cut in half before adding to soup.

"I got this recipe from some close friends several years ago. It's one you'll want to try."

Connie Sweet   **Rim of the World HS, Lake Arrowhead, CA**

Lasagna

Serves: 12 *Italy*

Meat Sauce:
1 1/2 pounds ground beef
3 (6 ounce) cans tomato paste
3 cups water
1/2 cup onion, finely chopped
1 clove garlic, minced
2 teaspoons salt
1/4 teaspoon pepper
3 bay leaves
1/2 teaspoon oregano
1 tablespoon dried parsley
1 (12 ounce) package lasagna noodles
1/2 cup parmesan cheese, grated
3/4 to 1 pound mozzarella, grated
1 pint ricotta cheese

Preheat oven to 350 degrees. Meat sauce: Brown meat in large skillet. Drain off excess fat. Combine tomato paste, water, onion, garlic, salt, pepper, bay leaves, oregano, and parsley. Add to meat. Cover and simmer for 1 hour. Remove bay leaves.

Assembling lasagna: Place lasagna noodles in a large pot of rapidly boiling salted water until al dente. Drain. Lay on paper towels. In a greased 9 x 13 pan, layer 1/3 of the meat sauce, 1/2 of the lasagna, 1/2 of the ricotta, and 1/3 of the mozzarella. Repeat layers. Finish with the remaining meat sauce, mozzarella, and the parmesan cheese. Bake for 40 minutes (1 1/4 hours if casserole has been refrigerated). Allow to stand about 5 minutes after removal from oven before cutting into squares and serving.

"Tried and true recipe given to me by my aunt, well before you could buy frozen lasagna. It is worth it to make it from scratch, but don't be afraid to add more garlic."

Sue Hope   **Lompoc HS, Lompoc, CA**

Linguine with Vegetables

Serves: 4-6   *Italy*

    1/2 pound linguine
    2 tablespoons butter or oil
    1 clove garlic, minced
    2 green onions, sliced
    2 small zucchini, ends trimmed and thinly sliced
    1/4 pound of mushrooms, sliced
    1 medium tomato, peeled and chopped
    1/2 teaspoon dried basil
    1/2 teaspoon salt
    1/4 teaspoon pepper
    1 cup provolone cheese, grated
    3 tablespoons Parmesan cheese, grated
    2 tablespoons parsley, chopped

Prepare all vegetables according to ingredient list. Cook pasta according to package directions. Drain in colander and return to pan. Heat butter or oil in large skillet. Add garlic, green onion, and zucchini. Sauté for 2 minutes. Add mushrooms and cook for 1 minute. Stir in tomatoes and seasonings. Reduce heat and simmer for 3 - 4 minutes or until vegetables are tender-crisp. Combine vegetables and cooked pasta. Add cheese and toss until cheese is melted. Sprinkle with parsley. Serve hot.

"This recipe comes from a former colleague, Roberta Marshall. It is a student favorite."

Cindy Peters   **Deer Valley HS, Antioch, CA**

Manicotti

Serves: 6   *Italy*

    3 cups store bought marinara sauce
    2 cups (1 pound) cottage cheese
    1 cup (4 ounces) shredded mozzarella cheese
    1/2 cup grated Parmesan cheese
    1/2 cup nonfat egg substitute
    1 teaspoon dried oregano
    1 teaspoon dried basil
    1 teaspoon salt
    1/2 teaspoon black pepper
    12 manicotti shells

Preheat oven to 350 degrees. Spray one 9 x 13 inch pan with nonstick cooking spray. Spread 1 cup of the marinara sauce on the bottom of the prepared baking dish. Set aside. In a large bowl, combine all the ingredients except the manicotti and stir until incorporated. Spoon the cheese mixture into the shells, dividing equally among them, and place the filled shells over the sauce in the baking dish. Spread the remaining marinara sauce evenly over the shells. Cover with foil and bake for 45 minutes to 1 hour. May make ahead and freeze. Thaw before baking as above.

"One of the most requested recipes for the new "Deals on Meals" program being offered by my students this year. Everyone loves this recipe!"

Jan Runyan   **Palm Desert Charter MS, Palm Desert, CA**

Meatball Minestrone Soup

Serves: 8   *Italy*

Meatballs:
10 ounces frozen chopped spinach
1 pound hamburger
1/2 pound sausage
1/3 cup bread crumbs
1 egg
1 teaspoon salt
1/2 teaspoon pepper
Soup:
1 large onion, chopped and sautéed
7 cups water
7 cubes beef bouillon
1 (16 ounce) can stewed tomatoes
1 (16 ounce) can kidney beans, include juice
1 teaspoon oregano
1 teaspoon basil
1 cup chopped carrots
1 cup chopped celery
1 cup pasta
1 small zucchini, diced

Mix together ingredients for meatballs. Brown, drain and set aside. (Cooking the meatballs on a cookie sheet in the oven is much easier than in a frying pan.) Mix first six soup ingredients in large saucepan. Simmer 10 minutes, then add carrots and celery. Simmer 10 more minutes. Add pasta and zucchini. Simmer 10 minutes more. Add meatballs and heat through. Serve sprinkled with grated Parmesan cheese.

"Better than what you get at Olive Garden!"

Julie Ericksen   **Skyline HS, Salt Lake City, CA**

Mediterranian Chicken Sandwiches

Serves: 4   *Italy*

4 sourdough sandwich rolls, toasted
2 chicken breasts
salt, pepper, garlic powder, to taste
1/2 cup store bought pesto sauce, divided
4 slices provolone cheese
8 slices tomatoes
4 slices cooked bacon
1/4 cup marinated artichoke hearts, chopped

Begin by splitting the sandwich rolls and toasting slightly. Cut the chicken breasts into inch strips. Sauté in a small amount of olive oil until no longer pink. Season with salt,

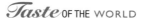

pepper, and garlic powder to taste. To assemble the sandwiches, spread 1 tablespoon of the pesto on each side of the sandwich roll. On the bottom half layer, 1/4 of the chicken pieces, tomatoes, artichoke hearts, and bacon. Top with cheese and run under broiler for a minute to melt the cheese. Slice and serve.

"This recipe started out as a thrown together creation from leftovers and has become a family favorite."

Delaine Smith   West Valley HS, Cottonwood, CA

Paella

Serves: 10   *Italy*

1/4 cup olive oil
4 pounds frying chicken pieces
1/4 cup all-purpose flour
1 teaspoon salt
1/8 teaspoon freshly ground pepper
1/4 cup water
1 teaspoon oregano
2 cups onion, chopped
2 cloves garlic, minced
3 tablespoons butter
2 cups uncooked long grain white rice
1/4 teaspoon powdered saffron
4 cups chicken stock
1/2 pound chorizo sausage, sliced
1 package frozen artichoke hearts, thawed
2 cups peas
1 (28 ounce) can tomatoes, drained and coarsely chopped
1 pound raw shrimp, shelled and deveined
1 (7 ounce) can pimientos, cut in strips
24 cherrystone clams

Preheat oven to 350 degrees. Heat olive oil in a large skillet with a cover. Dust chicken pieces with flour, salt, and pepper and brown well in oil. Add 1/4 cup water and oregano. Cover and cook for 30 minutes over low heat. Remove chicken and set aside. Add chopped onion and garlic to skillet and sauté, stirring, for 5 minutes. Set aside. In a saucepan, melt butter. Add rice and saffron. Stir over low heat for 5 minutes. Add chicken stock, cover and cook for 15 to 20 minutes. Stir rice into skillet with onions. In a separate skillet, brown chorizo sausage lightly. Set aside. In a 4-quart shallow casserole or pan, mix the artichoke hearts and peas with the rice, then lightly toss in the tomatoes, chorizo, and shrimp. Arrange the chicken pieces on top and garnish with pimientos. Bake, uncovered, for 30 minutes. Meanwhile, steam the clams in a separate container, discarding any that do not open, and place on top of casserole for last 3 to 5 minutes of baking.

Tracy Shannon   Swope MS, Reno, NV

Parmesan Chicken

Serves: 4-6   *Italy*

1 glove garlic, minced
1/2 cup butter, melted
1 cup dried bread crumbs
1/3 cup Parmesan cheese
2 tablespoons fresh parsley (2 teaspoons dried)
1/4 teaspoon garlic salt
pinch Italian seasoning
1/8 teaspoon ground black pepper
2 pounds chicken, boneless, skinless, cut into 2 x 2 inch pieces

Preheat oven to 450 degrees. In a bowl, combine minced garlic with the melted butter. In another bowl, mix together bread crumbs, Parmesan, parsley, garlic salt, Italian seasoning and pepper. Dip the chicken pieces into garlic butter, then into crumb mixture to coat. Place coated chicken pieces on a 9 x 13 inch baking dish; leave room between pieces. Drizzle with remaining garlic butter and bake uncovered 15 minutes or until chicken is cooked through and juices run clear. Note that the chicken will get more browned on the bottom side than on the top.

"We experimented with several chicken recipes and this was the students' favorite."

Margurite Simpson   **St. Helens HS, St. Helens, OR**

Pesto Sauce with Pasta

Serves: 4   *Italy*

1/3 cup basil leaves, coarsely chopped, packed
1/4 cup Parmesan cheese, grated
1/4 cup olive oil or vegetable oil
1/4 teaspoon pine nuts or walnuts
1/4 teaspoon salt
dash pepper
1 clove garlic
5 ounces spaghetti or noodles
1 tablespoon margarine or butter

Place all ingredients except pasta and margarine in blender container. Cover and blend on high speed until mixture is of uniform consistency. Cook pasta as directed on package, drain. Toss pasta with basil mixture and the margarine. Serve with additional Parmesan cheese, if desired.

"An easy dinner for the end to a busy day. Has a lot of Wow! to the meal.
Pesto sauce can be made and frozen in advance."

Maria Scirone, M.A.   **Westlake HS, Westlake, CA**

Polenta

Serves: 4-6   *Italy*

1 1/2 cups yellow cornmeal
1 cup cold water
4 cups boiling water
1 cup mozzarella, shredded
salt and pepper, to taste

Combine cornmeal and cold water in bowl. Stir to form paste. Add paste gradually to rapidly boiling water. Lower heat and stir constantly with wire whisk 10 minutes, or until mixture reaches a smooth consistency. Remove from heat and stir in cheese. Season with salt and pepper, to taste. Serve immediately with topping of choice. Topping examples: marinara sauce, spaghetti sauce, sautéed red or green peppers, sautéed eggplant, grated Parmesan cheese.

"My Italian Grandmother served Polenta with spaghetti sauce topped with Parmesan cheese; a family favorite."

Cheri Schuette   Valley View MS, Simi Valley, CA

Pork and Ricotta Meatballs

Serves: 8   *Italy*

Panco crumbs (used to your discretion for binding)
3/4 pound ground pork
3/4 pound lean ground beef
2 ounces pancetta, thickly sliced
3 large eggs
2/3 cup ricotta
1/4 cup parsley, chopped
1 teaspoon crushed oregano
1-4 teaspoons crushed red pepper
kosher salt
2 tablespoons basil, shredded
1/2 cup Romano cheese, fresh grated
2 (28 ounce) cans of crushed tomatoes
fresh ground pepper

Preheat oven to 400 degrees. Add pork, beef, pancetta and eggs, ricotta, 1 1/2 teaspoons kosher salt, basil and cheese. Mix well. Shape into 24+ meatballs, using about 3 tablespoons of mixture for each meatball. Roll each meatball in flour. Transfer to a slightly oiled baking sheet. Roast meatballs in the oven for 30 minutes or until firm and just beginning to brown. Using a spatula, loosen the meatballs from the bottom of the pan. Add the crushed tomato to the pan and season with salt and pepper. Lower the oven temperature to 350 degrees and cook uncovered for about 2 hours, or until sauce is very thick and meatballs are very tender; turn the meatballs once or twice during cooking.

"These can be made ahead of time. Before adding sauce, freeze them."

Dawn Maceyka   Great Oak HS, Temecula, CA

Roasted Red Pepper & Italian Sausage Penne

Serves: 4   *Italy*

6 red bell peppers, quartered, seeds and stems discarded
6 tablespoons Bertolli Extra Virgin Olive Oil
salt and freshly ground black pepper
1/2 cup Italian parsley leaves, packed
2 teaspoons dried oregano
1 tablespoon fresh thyme leaves, stripped from stem
2 cloves garlic, coarsely chopped
1 pound large white mushrooms, sliced
1 pound Italian sausage
1 pound penne or other tubular pasta shape
1/4 cup reserved pasta cooking liquid
grated Parmingiano-Reggiano, to taste

Heat oven to 450 degrees. Cut pepper quarters into 1/2 inch thick diagonal pieces. Place in 9 x 13 inch baking dish. Drizzle with 3 tablespoons olive oil; salt and pepper, to taste. Bake until peppers are charred on edges and tender, stir occasionally, 30-40 minutes. Remove from oven. Finely chop parsley, oregano, thyme and garlic together; set aside. Heat 3 tablespoons of oil in large nonstick skillet. Add mushrooms, cook, stirring, over medium high heat until mushrooms are tender and golden brown. Add chopped herb and garlic mixture; saute, stirring, 2 minutes. Sprinkle with salt and pepper, transfer to side dish. Wipe out skillet. Place sausage into skillet, cook, stirring, over medium high heat, until sausage is browned. Transfer to strainer, drain. To baking dish with roasted pepper, add mushroom mixture and sausage. Cover with foil. Keep warm in oven, set at lowest temperature. Boil large pot of water. Stir in penne, salt, to taste. Cook, stirring frequently, over high heat, until pasta is tender. Ladle out 1/4 cup pasta cooking liquid; reserve. Drain pasta. In a large deep platter combine pasta, red pepper, mushroom and sausage mixture. Stir to combine. Add pasta cooking liquid to moisten pasta. Sprinkle with cheese.

"My father brought this recipe home from Europe after World War II."

Dr. Terry Kluever   **Coronado HS, Las Vegas, NV**

Slow Cooker Lasagna

Serves: 4-6   *Italy*

1 pound lean ground beef ; 7% fat
1 small onion, chopped
1 medium clove garlic, minced
1 (28 ounce) can crushed tomatoes
1 (15 ounce) can tomato sauce
1 teaspoon salt
1 teaspoon dried oregano
1/2 teaspoon dried basil
1/4 teaspoon crushed red pepper flakes (optional)
1 cup part-skim ricotta cheese
1 1/2 cups part-skim mozzarella cheese, shredded
6 dry no-cook lasagna noodles broken in 1/2
1/2 cup Parmesan cheese, shredded

Heat a large nonstick skillet over medium-high heat. Add beef, onion, and garlic: cook stirring often, breaking up meat as it cooks, about 5-7 minutes. Stir in crushed tomatoes, tomato sauce, salt, oregano, basil, and pepper flakes: simmer 5 minutes. Meanwhile, in a medium bowl, stir ricotta cheese and 1 cup mozzarella. Spoon 1/3 of beef mixture into 5 quart slow cooker, 1/2 the noodles over the beef, 1/2 the ricotta, and repeat. Finish with beef. Cover slow cooker, cook on low 4-6 hours. In a small bowl, combine 1/2 cup mozzarella and Parmesan; sprinkle over beef. Cover and set aside until cheese melts and the lasagna firms up, about 10 minutes.

"This is a Weight Watchers recipe and is delicious."

Ruth Schletewitz   Rafer Johnson JHS, Kingsburg, CA

Summer Garden Pasta

Serves: 6   *Italy*

    3 cups cherry tomatoes, halved
    1/2 cup olive oil
    2 tablespoons minced garlic (6 cloves)
    18 large basil leaves, julienned
    1/2 teaspoon crushed red pepper flakes
    1 teaspoon kosher salt
    1/2 teaspoon freshly ground pepper
    1 pound dried angel hair pasta
    splash olive oil
    2 tablespoons kosher salt
    1 1/2 cups Parmesan cheese, freshly grated

Combine the cherry tomatoes, olive oil, garlic, basil leaves, red pepper flakes, 1 teaspoon salt and pepper in a large bowl. Cover with plastic wrap, and set aside at room temperature for about 4 hours. Just before you're ready to serve, bring a large pot of water with a splash of olive oil and 2 tablespoons salt to a boil and add pasta. Cook al dente according to the directions on the package. Drain the pasta well and add to the bowl with the cherry tomatoes. Add cheese and some extra basil leaves and toss well.

"This is a quick side dish or by adding some leftover chicken it could be a main course."

Linda Brayton   Grace Davis HS, Modesto, CA

Sun-Dried Tomato Risotto

Serves: 6   *Italy*

    4 1/2 cups vegetable broth + 1 tablespoon tomato chicken bouillon
    2 tablespoons butter
    1 tablespoon olive oil
    1/4 cup onion, diced
    3 cloves garlic, minced
    1 cup Arborio rice (do not rinse)
    1/4 cup sun-dried tomatoes, minced
    salt and pepper, to taste
    1/4 cup Parmesan, grated + 2 tablespoons for garnish
    4 fresh basil leaves, chopped, optional

Bring broth to a simmer in heavy small saucepan; reduce heat to low and keep hot. Heat butter and olive oil in a large pot or Dutch oven over medium heat. Add onions and garlic and cook 3-4 minutes until translucent. Add rice and stir 3 minutes. Add 1/2 cup stock; stir until almost absorbed, about 2 minutes. Add in minced sun-dried tomatoes and stir. Reduce heat to medium. Add 1 cup hot broth and cook until almost all liquid is absorbed, stirring often. Continue adding hot broth 1 cup at a time and stirring frequently until rice is almost tender, about 15 minutes. Remove from heat, and then stir in Parmesan. Season with salt and pepper as needed. Garnish with chopped basil and more Parmesan.

Lori Fuxa   **Rancho Alamitos HS, Garden Grove, Ca**

Tomato Basil Soup

Serves: 8   *Italy*

1 tablespoon olive oil
1 tablespoon garlic, chopped
1 (28 ounce) can crushed tomatoes
4 1/2 cups chicken broth
1/2 teaspoon red pepper flakes
1 bunch fresh basil for garnish
1/4 cup prepared pesto (optional)

Preheat olive oil in a 4 quart saucepan over medium high heat; add garlic and cook for 1-2 minutes until garlic is softened. Stir in the crushed tomatoes, chicken broth and red pepper flakes. Bring mixture to a boil and simmer for 20 minutes. While soup is cooking, rinse basil and dry on paper towels. Use kitchen shears to thinly slice the basil into small strips. After the 20 minute cooking time, stir the basil into the soup, heat thoroughly, and serve. If desired top each bowl with a spoonful of pesto.

"Serve the soup with a grilled cheese sandwich for the ultimate comfort food."

Beth Guerrero   **Selma HS, Selma, CA**

Tuscan Potato Soup

Serves: 4 - 6   *Italy*

1 pound hot Italian sausage
1 medium yellow onion, minced
1 (pound) package Applewood smoked bacon, chopped
5 1/2 cups chicken stock or broth
4-6 medium red potatoes, peel or leave on
1/2 teaspoon salt
1/2 teaspoon crushed red pepper flakes
2 cups half and half
4 cups kale, chopped

Sauté the Italian sausage (remove from casing), drain, and set aside. Then, sauté a minced onion with the apple wood smoked bacon. Add the chicken broth, potatoes, salt, red pepper flakes and cook on medium heat for about an hour, until the potatoes are cooked. Then add the sausage, cream, and chopped kale. Simmer until kale is softened. This soup works as a nice leftover, as well.

"A nice soup on a cold winter's day. A taste of Italy!!"

Donna Abbey   **Pleasant Valley HS, Chico, CA**

White Cheese Chicken Lasagna

Serves: 12   *Italy*

9 lasagna noodles, cooked
1/2 cup butter
1 onion, chopped
1 clove garlic, minced
1/2 cup all-purpose flour
2 cups chicken broth
1 1/2 cups milk
1/2 teaspoon salt
4 cups shredded mozzarella cheese, divided
1 cup Parmesan cheese, divided
1 teaspoon Italian seasoning
1/2 cup ground black pepper
2 cups ricotta cheese
2 cups cooked chicken meat, cubed
1 (10 ounce) package frozen chopped broccoli
1 tablespoon fresh parsley, chopped
1/4 cup grated Parmesan cheese, for topping

Preheat oven to 350 degrees. Melt the butter in a large saucepan over medium heat. Cook the onion and garlic in the butter until tender. Stir in the flour and salt and simmer until bubbly. Mix in broth and milk, until boiling. Boil mixture, stirring constantly for 1 minute. Stir in 2 cups mozzarella cheese and 1/4 cup Parmesan cheese. Season with Italian seasoning and black pepper. Remove from heat and set aside. Spread 1/3 of the sauce mixture in the bottom of a 9 x 13 in baking dish. Layer 1/3 of the noodles, the ricotta cheese, and the chicken. Continue layering 1/3 noodles, 1/3 of the sauce, broccoli and the remaining 2 cups mozzarella cheese and 1/2 cup Parmesan cheese. Arrange remaining noodles over cheese, and spread remaining sauce evenly over noodles. Sprinkle with parsley and 1/4 cup Parmesan cheese. Bake 35 to 40 minutes.

"A great dish to serve as an alternative to traditional lasagna. My family loves it."

Jeanette Atkinson   **Legacy HS, North Las Vegas, NV**

Caramel Apple Cake

Serves: 12   *Poland*

1 1/2 cups vegetable oil
1 1/2 cups sugar
1/2 cup packed brown sugar
3 eggs
3 cups flour
2 teaspoons cinnamon
1/2 teaspoon nutmeg
1 teaspoon baking soda
1/2 teaspoon salt
3 cups apples, finely diced and peeled
1 cup walnuts, chopped
2 teaspoons vanilla
Caramel Frosting:
1/2 cup brown sugar, packed
1/3 cup light cream
1/4 cup butter
1 dash salt
1 cup powdered sugar

Preheat oven to 325 degrees. Mix oil and sugars. Add eggs 1 at a time; beat well after each. Mix dry ingredients; add to batter and mix well. Fold in apples, walnuts and vanilla. Pour into greased and floured tube pan. Bake for 1 1/2 hours or until cake tests done. Cool. Frosting: Heat on low, brown sugar, cream, butter and salt until sugar is dissolved. Cool to room temperature. Beat in the powdered sugar until smooth; drizzle over the cake.

"Everyone loves this cake!"

Shirley Blanchard   Hanford West HS, Hanford, CA

Chrusciki (Sweet Crispy Pastry Ribbons)

Makes: about 8 dozen   *Poland*

1 tablespoon unsalted butter
2 large eggs
10 egg yolks
3 tablespoons sugar
1/2 teaspoon salt
1 teaspoon orange extract
1 teaspoon vanilla extract
1 teaspoon lemon rind, grated
1 teaspoon orange rind, grated
3 tablespoons whisky, rum, brandy or cognac (optional)
1/2 cup sour cream
4-5 cups flour
vegetable shortening for deep frying
powdered sugar, sifted for sprinkling

Melt butter and combine eggs, egg yolks, sugar, salt, extracts, citrus rind, alcohol and sour cream. Beat with a wooden spoon until thick and lemon colored. Gradually add enough flour to produce a fairly stiff dough. Turn onto a floured board and knead until dough blisters, becomes elastic, and can be handled easily adding flour if necessary; 8 to 10 minutes. Keep the bulk of the dough under an inverted bowl to prevent it from

drying out. Roll into small pieces of dough, very, very thin, and cut with a leaf-shaped cookie cutter. Heat the shortening to 375 degrees, and fry the dough leaves a few at a time until lightly browned, about 1 minute, turning once with tongs. To achieve slightly curved leaves, stretch the dough a bit as you drop it into hot shortening. Drain Chrushiki on brown paper bags, and sprinkle with powdered sugar. Store tightly covered in wax papered lined tins.

"Recipe can be adjusted to eliminate the alcohol. Replace the alcohol with 1 1/2 tsp each of vanilla and orange extract. For a total of 2 1/2 teaspoons each of vanilla and orange. I got this recipe from the Martha Stewart website. This makes an enormous quantity, so it can be halved but do not divide the orange or vanilla extracts."

Shirley Blanchard　　　　　　　　　Hanford West HS, Hanford, CA

Pierogi (Potato & Cheese Dumplings)
Makes: 3 dozen　　　　　　　　　　　　　　　　*Poland*

Filling: (make first)
2 cups mashed potatoes (do not add butter or milk)
1 cup dry cottage cheese (rinsed)
1 cup regular cottage cheese
1 egg
dash of salt and pepper
Dough:
4 cups flour
4 eggs
1 teaspoon salt
1 1/2 cups water

Mix filling ingredients all together in a bowl and set aside. Mix all dough ingredients then roll out like pie dough. Cut dough out with a 3" diameter water glass. Take a tablespoon of the filling, put in the middle of cut circles. Fold dough over filling so you now have a 1/2 circle. Press dough together so filling won't come out; use flour on your finger tips so dough won't stick to fingers. In a large pot of boiling water, gently drop in a few pirogi, but don't crowd them. Stir together so they won't stick to the bottom of pot. Stir for 5 minutes or until they start to float. Take them out of the pot and drain. Fry in butter then serve with melted butter.

Shirley Blanchard　　　　　　　　　Hanford West HS, Hanford, CA

Scottish Shortbread
Serves: 16-20　　　　　　　　　　　　　　　　*Scotland*

1 cup best-quality unsalted butter, softened (not melted)
1/2 cup sugar
1 1/2 cups all purpose flour, sifted
pinch salt

Preheat oven to 300 degrees. Lightly butter two 8 inch round cake pans or 1 13 x 9 inch rectangular pan; set aside. In a large bowl, cream the butter and sugar with a large wooden spoon, or knead with your hands for approximately 4 to 5 minutes. Mix the flour and salt in a small bowl; gradually add to the butter/sugar mixture, working each addition in completely. Use your hands (if you weren't already) to knead in the last bit of the dry ingredients. The dough will become lighter in color as you knead it. If using two cake pans, divide the dough in half, otherwise go ahead and press evenly into the bottom of the pan(s). Pierce the dough with a fork either randomly or in a pattern, but evenly spaced. Bake until shortbread is very pale gold (just browning around the edges) 28 to 30 minutes. Don't over-bake, or it will become dry and crumbly. Cool in the pan(s)on a cooling rack for 5 to 10 minutes. While it is still somewhat warm, carefully cut into wedges (if in cake pans) or 1 inch squares (if in rectangular pan). After completely cooled, wrap tightly in tin foil or tins (you can layer it with waxed paper in between layers). Aging the shortbread for a week or more enhances the flavor.

"My father's family is Scottish and we go to the Scottish games every year for a family reunion. Shortbread is a necessary ingredient for a successful gathering of the clans!"

Mary Makela   **Fort Bragg HS, Fort Bragg, CA**

Spanish Breakfast Strata
Serves: 8   *Spain*

    12 large eggs, beaten until fluffy
    1 loaf French bread, broken into small pieces
    2 cups cooked ham (sausage or bacon), chopped
    1 medium onion, chopped
    1 (4 ounce) can green chilies, chopped
    1 (10.5 ounce) can cream mushroom soup
    1 (14.5 ounce) can evaporated milk
    2 cups shredded Jack and cheddar cheese (save for later)

Mix all of the above together (except the cheese) and pour into a 9 x 13 buttered baking dish. Refrigerate overnight. Bake at 350 for 50 minutes until center is firm. 10 minutes before strata is finished add cheese and cover with foil.

"Can be found at most holiday breakfast tables, in my family. :)"

Julie Carriere   **North Monterey County HS, Castroville, CA**

Tortilla Espanola
Serves: 4   *Spain*

    3 large eggs
    salt and pepper, tö taste
    3 to 4 tablespoons olive oil
    3 large potatoes, peeled and thinly sliced
    1 onion, peeled and finely chopped
    green olives, for garnish

Crack the eggs into a large bowl. Whisk with a fork and add a pinch of salt. Heat oil in a large frying pan on medium- high heat. Add the potatoes and fry for 2-3 minutes. Add the onion and stir together. When the potatoes start to brown a little on the edges, mash slightly with the onion until the mixture is lumpy. Then add the eggs. Make sure the potatoes and onions are fully submerged by the eggs. Poke the potatoes to allow some of the egg to seep into the mashed mixture. Reduce the heat to low. While cooking, shake the pan to loosen the "tortilla" from the base and gently push down the sides with a wooden spoon. Do not over cook. The middle will remain a little runny and gooey. As the egg begins to set, place a pan or plate over the entire pan. Quickly flip the tortilla over onto the plate and slide back into the pan to cook the underside. Keep shaking the pan lightly so the tortilla does not stick to the bottom. Once it feels firm on the edges and soft in the middle (after 1-2 minutes), slide the tortilla back onto

a plate. Let it rest for 5 minutes before slicing into wedges to serve. Garnish with green olives.

"Great served open-faced on a slice of French or sourdough bread!"

Amanda Speake   Ponderosa HS, Shingle Springs, CA

Cevapcici (Yugoslavian Sausages)

Serves: 6-8   *Yugoslavia*

1 pound ground hamburger
1/2 pound ground pork
1/2 large red onion, peeled and finely chopped
3 cloves garlic, peeled and finely chopped
3 teaspoons sweet paprika
a little cayenne
2 teaspoons black pepper, freshly ground
1/4 bunch fresh mint, finely chopped
1/2 bunch fresh parsley, finely chopped
1 egg
1/2 cup plain bread crumbs
salt, to taste
olive oil, for basting
Kamak:
8 ounces cream cheese
4 ounces crumbled feta cheese
1 stick butter

Mix all the ingredients, except the oil, thoroughly and roll the mixture into little "cigars" about 1 x 3 inches (or meat balls). Rub lightly with olive oil and grill or broil until done. These are great on the barbecue. Serve with Kamak. Kamak: Place all ingredients in food processor and blend until velvety smooth. Chill to firm. Serve over hot French bread with roasted garlic and Cevapcici.

Stephanie San Sebastian   Central HS, Fresno, CA

India

· ·

Carol's Chicken Curry

Serves: 6   *India*

2 large chicken breasts with bones
3 cups water
1 bay leaf
1 carrot, whole with skin left on
3 celery stalks with tops left on (can be celery hearts)
2 peppercorns
1/2-1 whole onion, chopped
3 tablespoons butter or margarine
3 tablespoons flour
1/2 teaspoon sugar
1 tablespoon curry powder
1/8 teaspoon cinnamon
1/4 teaspoon ginger
1 teaspoon salt
1 green apple, chopped
1 stalk celery, diced
1 carrot, peeled and diced
1/2 cup seedless raisins
1 cup half and half
steamed white rice for serving
Optional condiments: any flavor chutney, toasted coconut, sieved boiled eggs,
    chopped peanuts, fried and crumbled bacon, green onions, diced candied ginger

In a 2 quart saucepan, bring chicken breasts to a boil in water. Add bay leaf, unpeeled carrot, 3 celery stalks with tops, and peppercorns to the water. Reduce to a simmer and allow to cook until chicken is done (threads with a fork). Reserve broth. Allow meat to cool, remove chicken meat from bones. Cut chicken into bite sized pieces. Strain chicken broth, reserving for directions noted in recipe below. In a separate large skillet, sauté onion in butter until golden brown. Whisk in flour, sugar, curry powder, cinnamon, ginger and salt. Add 2 cups of chicken broth slowly and whisk until slightly thickened. Add apple pieces, celery, carrots and raisins. Cook over low heat for 7-10 minutes. Add cooked chicken and stir to coat. Add half and half and cook 3-4 more minutes. Serve with steamed rice and any of the chosen condiments listed above.

"This is a family recipe my mother, Carol Dziedzic got while we were an Air Force family living overseas. It isn't too strong for folks trying curry for the first time. My students are always surprised how good it is. Must get chutney for a topping! It is a very traditional tasty condiment with the consistency of jam."

Patti Bartholomew   **Casa Roble HS, Orangevale, California**

Carrot Slaw with Cashews
Serves: 6   *India*

3 cups carrots, finely shredded
1 quart boiling water
1/2 serrano chile, seeded and minced
2 tablespoons fresh lime juice
1 1/2 tablespoons maple syrup
2 tablespoons chopped cashews, pan-toasted until lightly golden
1 tablespoon cilantro, finely chopped

Place the carrots in a colander and pour boiling water over them and drain well.
Combine the chile, lime juice, and maple syrup in a bowl and whisk with a fork. Add
the carrots, cashews, and cilantro and toss to mix. Serve at room temperature or
chilled.

Cherri Farrell   **College Park HS, Pleasant Hill, CA**

Chicken Tikka Masala
Serves: 4 -6   *India*

Chicken:
1/2 teaspoon ground cumin
1/2 teaspoon ground coriander
1/4 teaspoon cayenne
1 teaspoon table salt
2 pounds boneless, skinless chicken breasts, trimmed of fat
1 cup plain whole-milk yogurt
2 tablespoons vegetable oil
2 medium garlic cloves, minced or pressed through garlic press
1 tablespoon fresh ginger, grated
Masala Sauce (can be made 4 days ahead of time):
3 tablespoons vegetable oil
1 medium onion, diced fine (about 1 1/4 cups)
2 medium garlic cloves, minced
2 teaspoons grated fresh ginger
1 serrano chile, ribs and seeds removed, flesh minced (or leave ribs
    and seeds in if you like it spicier)
1 tablespoon tomato paste
1 tablespoon garam masala
1 (28 ounce) can crushed tomatoes
2 teaspoons sugar
1/2 teaspoon table salt
2/3 cup heavy cream
1/4 cup fresh cilantro leaves, chopped

Chicken: Combine cumin, coriander, cayenne and salt in small bowl. Sprinkle both
sides of chicken with spice mixture, pressing gently so mixture adheres. Place chicken
on a plate, cover with plastic wrap and refrigerate for 30 to 60 minutes. In large bowl,
whisk together yogurt, oil, garlic and ginger; set aside. *Sauce:* Heat oil in large Dutch
oven over medium heat until shimmering. Add onion and cook, stirring frequently, until
light golden, 8-10 minutes. Add garlic, ginger, chile, tomato paste and garam masala;
cook, stirring frequently until fragrant, about 3 minutes. Add crushed tomatoes, sugar
and salt; bring to a boil. Reduce heat to medium-low, cover, and simmer for 15
minutes stirring occasionally. Stir in cream and return to simmer. Remove pan from

heat and cover to keep warm. While sauce simmers, adjust oven rack to upper-middle position (about 6 inches from heating element) and heat broiler. Using tongs, dip chicken into yogurt mixture (chicken should be covered with thick layer of yogurt) and arrange on wire rack set in foil lined rimmed baking sheet or broiler pan. Discard excess yogurt mixture. Broil chicken until thickest parts register 160 degrees and exterior is lightly charred in spots, 10-18 minutes, flipping chicken halfway through cooking. Let chicken rest 5 minutes, then cut into 1 inch chunks and stir into warm sauce (do not simmer chicken in sauce). Stir in cilantro, adjust seasoning with salt and serve.

"Sauce is amazing; the flavors are close to eating in an Indian restaurant. Add anything to it: spinach, peas, whatever you want. Serve with Naan bread and Basmati rice."

Cheryl Moyle   **Olympus HS, Salt Lake City, UT**

Coconut Dal

Serves: 4   *India*

1 small yellow onion, chopped finely
2 garlic cloves, chopped
1 dash of olive oil
2 cups yellow split peas
1 (14 ounce) can light coconut milk
4 cups low sodium vegetable broth (possibly more)
1 tablespoon fresh ginger, grated
2 teaspoons turmeric
1 teaspoon kosher salt
fresh cilantro, chopped, for garnish
Optional: toasted fresh coconut for garnish

Sauté the onion and garlic in a small bit of olive oil in a saucepan. Add the coconut milk, vegetable broth, peas, and spices. Mix and bring to a simmer. Simmer uncovered about 30 minutes, or until peas are tender and it begins to thicken. The liquid should be absorbed and the peas soft-tender. If you want this dish with less texture, you can add more broth and cook a bit longer. Garnish with cilantro and/or fresh toasted coconut.

"This recipe was adapted from the book, "UltraMetabolism" - it is hearty, healthy, tasty, and very pretty on the plate."

Amy Bean   **Lompoc HS, Lompoc, CA**

Curried Red Lentil Soup with Baby Spinach

Serves: 6-8   *India*

2 tablespoons extra virgin olive oil
1 large onion, diced
2/3 cup thinly sliced carrots
3 cloves garlic, minced
6 teaspoons curry powder
1 teaspoon ground fenugreek
1/2 teaspoon ground cayenne
3 cups vegetable broth
3 cups water
1 pound red lentils
1 (15 ounce) can garbanzo beans, drained and rinsed
3 1/12 cups packed baby spinach
kosher salt to taste, optional

Heat olive oil in a large pot over medium heat. Sauté the onion and carrots for about 10 minutes. Add the garlic, curry powder, fenugreek, and cayenne, and sauté for about 30 seconds. Add the broth and water and increase heat to high. Bring to a boil. Add lentils and garbanzos and reduce heat to medium. Cover the pot with a lid and simmer for about 8 minutes, stirring occasionally. Add spinach and cook for 2 minutes more, or until wilted. Season with salt, if desired.

"This thick, quick-cooking soup is healthy and smells amazing. Red lentils turn yellow when cooked. Using red lentils allows this soup to cook up quickly."

Margo Olsen   Amador Valley and Foothill HS, Pleasanton, CA

Homemade Naan

Makes: 4 large pieces of Naan   *India*

2/3 cup hot milk
2 teaspoons granulated sugar, divided
2 teaspoons active dried yeast
4 cups flour
1/2 teaspoon salt
1 teaspoon baking powder
2 tablespoons vegetable oil
1 large egg, lightly beaten
2/3 cup plain yogurt, lightly beaten
vegetable spray or 1/4 teaspoon oil

Pour hot milk into a bowl and add 1 teaspoon sugar and yeast. Stir to mix and set aside for 15-20 minutes. Sift flour, salt and baking powder into a large bowl. Add the remaining 1 teaspoon of sugar, vegetable oil, egg, yogurt, and the yeast mixture. Mix and knead to form a ball of dough. Place the dough on a clean work surface and knead for 10 minutes. Pour about 1/4 teaspoon oil into large bowl and roll the dough in it or spray with vegetable spray. Cover with plastic wrap and set in a warm place until double the volume. On a cutting board, cut dough in 1/2, then 1/2 again. Working with one piece at a time, with the other pieces under the plastic, roll to 6-7 inch diameter and set aside. Repeat with 3 other pieces. Heat oven to 500 degrees with baking stone on middle shelf. Place bread dough on parchment paper and place on stone using pizza paddle. Bake 3-5 minutes. Repeat with other 3 dough pieces. Keep warm in a cloth.

"Naan tastes great with Chicken Masala and Basmati rice."

Cheryl Moyle   **Olympus HS, Salt Lake City, UT**

Mohini's Chicken Curry
Serves: 3-4   *India*

    2 tablespoons unsalted butter
    1/2 onion, finely chopped
    1-2 cloves garlic, minced
    1 tomato, finely chopped
    1 1/2 tablespoons curry powder, or to taste
    1/2 teaspoon salt, or to taste
    pinch sugar
    1 pound chicken breast, cut into 1-inch pieces
    1/4 cup cilantro, chopped
    1/2 cup half & half or cream

In large skillet or pot, melt butter; add onion, garlic and tomatoes and sauté about 2 minutes. Stir in curry powder, salt & sugar. Add chicken and cilantro and cook on medium heat, stirring, until chicken is done. Add cream and simmer on low heat for 2 minutes.

"Mohini is a THS graduate who is a self-taught personal chef and has launched a line of her own specialty spices sold in several local stores and on-line at indianfusions.com."

Laura de la Motte   **Turlock HS, Turlock, CA**

Mulligatawny Soup
Serves: 5   *India*

    1/4 cup canola oil
    1/4 cup yellow onion, finely diced
    1/4 cup celery, finely diced
    1/4 cup Granny Smith apple, peeled and diced
    1/4 banana, peeled and diced
    1/2 tablespoon garlic, minced
    1 1/2 tablespoons flour
    4 cups chicken stock
    3/4 cup Major Grey's Mango Chutney
    1 1/2 tablespoons Madras curry powder
    1 cup heavy cream
    2 cups basmati rice, cooked
    6 ounces chicken meat, cooked and medium diced
    salt and pepper, to taste

Heat oil. Add onion and celery and cook until tender. Add apples and cook until apples start to soften. Add bananas and garlic; after the bananas soften, add flour and cook for about 10 minutes. Add chicken stock, bring to simmer and add chutney and curry, which have been mixed together. Cook until apples are completely tender and then blend until smooth. Add heavy cream, mix well. Add chicken and rice. Simmer for about 10 minutes. Adjust seasoning with salt and more curry, if desired.

Scott Domeny   **Del Oro HS, Loomis, CA**

Mustard Grill's Curried Slaw

Serves: 4 to 8   *India*

Curry Vinaigrette:
2 tablespoons prepared Indian curry paste
1 tablespoon Dijon mustard
2 tablespoons lemon juice
2 tablespoons rice vinegar
1/4 teaspoon salt
3/4 teaspoon freshly ground pepper
1/4 cup plus 2 tablespoons extra virgin oil
Slaw:
4 cups thinly sliced green cabbage(about 1/3 head)
1 carrot, peeled and grated
1 jalapeno chile, seeded and thinly sliced
prepared vinaigrette
1/4 cup fresh cilantro leaves
2 green onions, white and light green parts, thinly sliced on the diagonal

In a medium bowl, whisk together the curry paste, mustard, lemon juice, rice vinegar,salt and pepper until the salt is dissolved, about 30 seconds. Gradually whisk in the olive oil, and continue to whisk until fully emulsified. This makes a scant cup of vinaigrette, which will keep for up to 3 days, covered and refrigerated. Slaw and assembly: In a large bowl, toss together the cabbage, carrot, and chile. Stir the vinaigrette to make sure it is emulsified and toss the slaw with just enough to coat lightly; you may not use all of the vinaigrette. Place the slaw in a serving bowl or divide onto plates. Garnish the bowl or servings with the cilantro leaves and green onion.

"This is a recipe from Mustard Grill in Napa, CA. Curry paste comes in mild and hot. You can find it in many supermarkets or in Asian markets. This slaw is delicious with added cooked chicken or shrimp as a main dish salad."

Betty Rabin-Fung, Retired   **Sierra Vista JHS, Canyon Country, CA**

Samosas

Serves: 4-6   *India*

1 large onion, finely chopped
1-2 cloves garlic, finely chopped
1 teaspoon curry powder
1/2 red or green pepper, finely chopped (optional)
cooking oil
1 package wonton skins
1 pound ground beef

Sauté onions, garlic, curry powder and peppers in a small amount of oil. Add meat to sautéed mixture. Cook mixture thoroughly; drain fat. Place a small spoonful of meat mixture in the center on wonton skin. Wet edges of wonton skin with water, fold into a triangle; press edges. Deep-fry a few samosas at a time. Turn them in oil. When samosas are a light golden brown color, remove and drain on a paper towel.

"Samosas are good hot or cold. They can be frozen before or after frying."

Carrie Smith   **Royal HS, Simi Valley, CA**

Islands

• •

Pollo de Coco (Caribbean Coconut Chicken)

Serves: 4   *Caribbean*

4 skinless, boneless chicken breasts
2 teaspoons vegetable oil
1 small onion, chopped
1 red bell pepper, chopped
1 green bell pepper, chopped
1 tablespoon roasted garlic, chopped
1 (14 ounce) can coconut milk
salt and pepper, to taste
1 pinch crushed red pepper flakes

Preheat oven to 425 degrees. In a large skillet, fry the chicken breasts in vegetable oil until the chicken just begins to brown. Stir the onions and bell peppers into the skillet with the chicken. Sauté until the onions are translucent. When the vegetables are translucent, add the garlic and coconut milk. Stir gently. Let the mixture cook 5 to 8 minutes. Remove the skillet from the heat. Season with a hint of salt, pepper, and red pepper flakes. Transfer the mixture to a 9 x 13 inch baking dish. Bake for 45 minutes, or until the vegetables cook down and the chicken is tender. Serve with rice and black beans.

"This is an aromatic, flavorful dish that is sure to please. Buen provecho!"

Holly Ebnit   Whittier Christian HS, La Habra, CA

Hawaiian Delight Cake

Makes: 1   *Hawaii*

Cake:
1 yellow cake mix
4 eggs
2/3 cup oil
3/4 cup water
1 (3.4 ounce) package orange Jell-O
1/2 cup coconut
1 (8 ounce) can crushed pineapple, drained
Icing:
4 ounces cream cheese, softened
1 stick butter, softened
1 cup powdered sugar

Preheat oven to 350 degrees. Mix all cake ingredients together thoroughly by hand or with mixer. Bake in greased and floured bundt pan for 50 minutes. Cool to warm and invert on a plate. Ice the cooled cake.

"Found this recipe in a newspaper while visiting Hawaii. Soooo simple. Aloha!"

Karyn Hobbs   Lemoore HS, Lemoore, CA

Hawaiian Lumpia

Serves: 6   *Hawaii*

1/4 pound ground beef
1/4 pound ground pork
2 garlic cloves, minced
1/2 small onion, minced
1/4 can chopped Spam (3 ounces)
1 stalk celery, chopped
1 carrot, chopped
1/4 can water chestnuts, chopped (2 ounces)
1/4 package bean sprouts, chopped (3 ounces)
salt, pepper and red pepper flakes
Lumpia wrappers
Peanut Dipping Sauce (see recipe)

Cook ground beef and pork with garlic and onion; drain. Add Spam, chopped celery and carrots and water chestnuts. When Spam, carrots, celery and onion are cooked, add bean sprouts. Season with salt, pepper and red pepper flakes.
To wrap Lumpia: Place single wrapper on flat surface. Place 2 heaping tablespoonfuls of filling on wrapper about 1/2 from bottom and center. Fold over bottom of wrapper over filling. Fold both sides in. Continue rolling until it reaches the top edge of wrapper. Moisten edges; finished roll should look like a log. Fry Lumpia in 1/2 inch of oil. Drain well by elevating one end on paper towels. Makes about 20 Lumpia.
"Spam you say?... don't be put off by this addition. Students really like trying something they have heard of but never tasted. Try the peanut dipping sauce, it's amazing."
Jackie Lawson   Dublin HS, Dublin, CA

Hawiian Ham Sandwiches

Makes: 24   *Hawaii*

24 King's Hawaiian rolls
24 slices honey ham (can also use turkey)
24 slices Swiss cheese
1/3 cup mayonnaise
1/3 cup Miracle Whip
1 1/2 tablespoons poppy seeds
1 1/2 tablespoons yellow mustard
1/2 cup butter, melted
1 tablespoon minced onion
1/2 teaspoon Worcestershire sauce

Preheat oven to 350 degrees. In small bowl, mix together mayonnaise and Miracle Whip. Split rolls and spread mayonnaise mixture on both halves. Place a slice of ham and a slice of cheese on each roll. Close rolls and place them very close together in a large baking dish or jelly roll pan. In a medium bowl, whisk together: poppy seeds, mustard, butter, onion and Worcestershire sauce. Pour sauce evenly over all sandwiches. Let sit for 10 minutes or until butter sets up slightly. Cover pan with foil and bake for 12 - 15 minutes or until cheese is melted. Uncover and cook for an additional 2 minutes. Serve warm.
"Hawaiian rolls are delicious by themselves but when used to make these sandwiches they add that extra sweetness. This recipe is a unique way to use your leftover holiday ham."
Barbara Correia   Foothill HS, Pleasanton, CA

Macadamia Nut Creme Pie

Serves: 8   *Hawaii*

3 egg yolks
3 cups milk
3/4 cup sugar
1/3 cup cornstarch
1/2 teaspoon salt
2 tablespoons butter
1 1/2 teaspoons vanilla extract
1 cup macadamia nuts, roasted and chopped
1 baked pie shell

Combine first 6 ingredients in sauce pan over medium, heat, stirring constantly. Boil for 1 minute and remove from heat; stir in vanilla and macadamia nuts. Pour into pie shell, cover with plastic and chill.

"Very simple and quick. Every year while in Hawaii we have this pie at one of our favorite restaurants. This restaurant is kind enough to share this recipe. Aloha."

Karyn Hobbs   Lemoore HS, Lemoore, CA

Macadamia Nut Pancakes

Serves: 8-10 Pancakes   *Hawaii*

1 cup all-purpose flour
1 tablespoon sugar
2 teaspoons baking powder
1/4 teaspoon salt
1/2 cup macadamia nuts, finely chopped
1 egg, beaten
1 cup milk
2 tablespoons vegetable oil
1/2 cup macadamia nuts, coarsely chopped

Lightly oil a griddle or skillet, heat until a drop of water skittles across the surface. In a medium size mixing bowl, stir together flour, sugar, baking powder, salt and finely chopped macadamia nuts. In a small mixing bowl, combine egg, milk and vegetable oil. Make a well in the middle of the dry ingredients and add the liquid ingredients all at once. Stir mixture just until blended but still slightly lumpy. Pour about 1/4 cup batter onto the hot griddle for a standard sized pancake. Cook until pancakes are golden brown, turning to cook second side when pancakes have a bubbly surface and slightly, dry edges. Sprinkle some of the coarsely chopped macadamia nuts on top and serve with hot syrup.

"So good! Always reminds me of my college days in Hawaii!"

Linda A. Stokes   Riverton HS, Riverton, UT

Mango Yogurt Parfaits
Makes: 6
France

2 large ripe mangos, peeled, pitted and cubed
3 cups low fat vanilla yogurt
6 tablespoons low fat granola

Puree 1 mango and spoon equal amounts into 6 clear plastic cups. Top each with 1/4 cup yogurt. Spoon cubed mango over the top, saving a few pieces for garnish. Top with remaining 1/4 cup yogurt and reserved mango. (Recipe may be made ahead at this point. Cover and refrigerate until ready to serve.) Top each serving with a tablespoon of granola just before serving.

Photo ©2008 National Mango Board and used by permission of the National Mango Board. All rights reserved.

Mango Yogurt Parfait

Cappuccino Brownie
with Wisconsin
Mascarpone Cheese

Tiramisu Cheesecake
with Wisconsin
Mascarpone Cheese

Cappuccino Brownies with Wisconsin Mascarpone Cheese

Serves: 9   *Italy*

Brownies:
1 1/2 tablespoons freeze-dried coffee
2 tablespoons boiling water
1 package (21 to 24 ounces)
    brownie mix
3/4 cup sour cream
1/4 cup butter, melted
2 eggs

Topping:
1 8-ounce container Wisconsin
    Mascarpone Cheese,
    at room temperature
1/2 cup whipping cream, whipped
2 tablespoons confectioners' sugar
1/2 teaspoon vanilla
Jimmies, cocoa or bittersweet
    chocolate shavings for garnish

For the brownies: Preheat oven to 350°F. Dissolve coffee in boiling water in large bowl. Add brownie mix, sour cream, melted butter and eggs; mix well. Spread the batter into buttered 9 x 9 baking pan. Bake for about 25-30 minutes, or until the brownies begin to pull away from the sides of the pan, (do not over bake.) Cool completely on rack. For the topping: Stir Mascarpone until soft, add whipping cream, sugar and vanilla. Continue stirring until mixture is smooth. Cut brownies into 3-inch squares and pipe or spoon Mascarpone cheese mixture on tops. Garnish with optional jimmies, cocoa or bittersweet chocolate shavings. Cover lightly and refrigerate until serving time.

Wisconsin Milk Marketing Board   **WisDairy.com**

Tiramisu Cheesecake with Wisconsin Mascarpone Cheese

Serves: 8   *Italy*

Crust:
1 1/2 cups biscotti cookie crumbs
3 tablespoons unsalted butter, melted
1 teaspoon instant espresso granules
Filling:
3 cups (12 ounces) Wisconsin
    Ricotta cheese
1 cup (4 ounces) Wisconsin
    Mascarpone cheese

1 tablespoon instant espresso granules
1 cup sugar
1/4 cup flour
4 eggs
1 tablespoon brandy, optional
1 teaspoon pure vanilla extract
1 1/2 cups mini-chocolate chips
Cocoa powder for dusting
Chocolate-covered coffee beans

Preheat oven to 350°F. Combine crumbs, butter and espresso granules; mix well. Press into and up the sides of a 9-inch spring form pan; set aside. Beat together Ricotta cheese, Mascarpone cheese, espresso granules, sugar and flour. In another bowl, combine eggs, brandy and vanilla. Add to cheese mixture and blend thoroughly. Fold in chocolate chips. Pour batter into prepared crust and bake at for 1 hour and 15 minutes (top will be slightly loose). Turn off oven and let cake cool in oven for 30 minutes. Remove from oven; cool completely. Refrigerate overnight. Remove sides from springform pan and sprinkle cake with cocoa powder, if desired. Garnish with coffee beans before serving.

Wisconsin Milk Marketing Board   **WisDairy.com**

Peanut Dipping Sauce

Serves: 6   *Hawaii*

1/3 cup crunchy or smooth peanut butter
2 tablespoons soy sauce
1 teaspoon white sugar
2 drops hot pepper sauce or oil
2 cloves garlic, minced
1 tablespoon sesame oil
1 tablespoon minced ginger
1/2 cup water
sliced green onions and sesame seeds for garnish

In a small bowl, stir together all ingredients except water. Gradually stir in water until texture is smooth and creamy.

"Use with the Hawaiian Lumpia."

Jackie Lawson   Dublin HS, Dublin, CA

Toasted Coconut Dessert

Serves: 12   *Hawaii*

Crust:
1/3 cup brown sugar
1 cup flour
1/2 cup butter, melted
1 cup slivered almonds
1 1/4 cups coconut
Filling:
1 (3 ounce) package vanilla instant pudding
1 (3 ounce) package coconut instant pudding
2 2/3 cups cold milk
2 cups Cool Whip

Preheat oven to 350 degrees. Mix all crust ingredients together in 9 x 13 inch baking pan and bake for 25 - 30 minutes; stirring every 10 minutes. Allow to cool. Take out 1 cup of this mixture to sprinkle on the top and spread the remaining in the bottom of the pan. To make the filling: make the puddings together with the milk. After it has thickened, fold in the Cool Whip. Pour over the crust. Sprinkle the remaining 1 cup crust on top. Chill and enjoy!

"This is a must if you love coconut. Yummy, yummy, yummy!"

Gay Quinn   Jordan HS, Sandy, UT

Pina Colada Sorbet

Serves: 8   *Puerto Rico*

1 1/2 cups white sugar
1 1/2 cups water
1 (20 ounce) can canned crushed pineapple, drained
1 (13.5 ounce) can coconut milk
1/4 cup lime juice

Make a syrup by bringing the sugar and water to a boil in a small saucepan over high heat, stir and boil until the liquid becomes clear, about 1 minute. Set aside to cool. Blend the drained pineapple in a blender or food processor until very smooth and frothy. In a large bowl, whisk together the syrup, pineapple puree, coconut milk and lime juice. Refrigerate until chilled, about 3 hours. Freeze in the freezer canister of an ice cream maker according to the manufacturer's directions.

Diana Lee   David Brown MS, Wildomar, CA

Tostones

Serves: 8   *Puerto Rico*

1/4 cup vegetable oil
3 green plantains, peeled, and cut into 1-inch pieces
1 pinch garlic powder
salt to taste

Heat the oil in a large skillet over medium heat. Add the plantain slices and fry until they soften, 5 to 10 minutes. Remove from the oil and drain on paper towels. Use a tostonera (a press) to slightly mash each piece until it is about 1/2 inch thick. If you do not have a tostonera, use a mallet or place the pieces between a folded paper bag and press down with a saucer. Press all of the pieces before going onto the next step. Return the pieces to the hot skillet and fry until crispy, about 3 minutes per side. Drain on paper towels and season with garlic powder and salt while still warm.

Diana Lee   David Brown MS, Wildomar, CA

• •

Jewish Bread (Challah)

Makes: 1 loaf   *Israel*

1 1/4 cups warm water (110 degrees)
2 teaspoons active dry yeast
1/4 cup sugar
1 tablespoon honey
4 tablespoons vegetable oil
2 eggs
1/2 tablespoon salt
4 cups unbleached all-purpose flour
1 tablespoon poppy seeds (optional)

Preheat oven to 375 degrees. In a large bowl, sprinkle yeast and sugar over barely warm water. Beat in honey, oil, eggs, and salt. Add the flour one cup at a time, beating after each addition, graduating to kneading with hands as dough thickens. Knead until smooth and elastic and no longer sticky, adding flour as needed. Cover with a damp clean cloth and let rise for 1 1/2 hours or until dough has doubled in bulk. (Refrigerate until the next day) Punch down the risen dough and turn out onto floured board. Divide in half and knead each half for five minutes or so, adding flour as needed to keep from getting sticky. Divide each half into thirds and roll into long snake about 1 1/2 inches in diameter. Pinch the ends of the three snakes together firmly and braid from middle. Either leave as braid or form into a round braided loaf by bringing ends together, curving braid into a circle, pinch ends together. Grease two baking trays and place finished braid or round on each. Cover with towel and let rise about one hour. Beat the remaining egg and brush a generous amount over each braid. Sprinkle with poppy seeds if desired. Bake for about 40 minutes. Bread should have a nice hollow sound when thumped on the bottom. Cool on a rack for at least one hour before slicing.

"This is an easy recipe to vary; chocolate, raspberry, vanilla bean, sesame are a few favorite variations. A rich egg bread traditional at Jewish Sabbath."

Priscilla Burns   **Pleasant Valley HS, Chico, CA**

Mama Goldman's Noodle Krugel

Serves: 12   *Israel*

12 ounces wide egg noodles
2 eggs, slightly beaten
1/4 cup sugar
1 cube margarine, melted
zest of one orange
1 quart buttermilk
Topping:
1 cube margarine, melted
3/4 cup corn flakes, crushed (I've been known to use more.)
1/4 cup sugar

Preheat oven to 350 degrees. Drain boiled noodles; mix with other ingredients (except buttermilk). Grease large 9 x 13 inch pan. Pour mixture in. Pour buttermilk over mixture and let stand overnight. Combine topping ingredients. Top noodles with mixture. Bake for 1 1/2 hours. Enjoy!

"A traditional dish served during the High Holy Days,
this Noodle Krugel dish has also accompanied my son and his bride's wedding dinner."

Dianne Lee Goldman   Cordova HS, Rancho Cordova, CA

Eggplant Casserole

Serves: 6   *Lebanon*

1 stick butter (1/4 pound)
1 pound ground beef or lamb
1 onion, chopped
1/2 cup pine nuts
dash of allspice, nutmeg, and cinnamon
salt and pepper to taste
oil pan spray
2 large eggplants, peeled and sliced lengthwise
1 (12 - 14 ounce) can of tomato sauce

Preheat oven to 350. Melt butter in pan and sauté the beef (or lamb), onion, pine nuts, and all spices until slightly browned. Set to one side. Meanwhile, place eggplant slices on an oiled cookie sheet and place under broiler until lightly browned and soft. Spray a 9 x 13 inch dish and place one layer of eggplant on the bottom of the dish. Cover with the meat mixture. Add a second layer of eggplant to cover the meat mixture. Cover the entire casserole with the can of tomato sauce and bake for 30 minutes, until bubbly.

"This is from Gramma Marie."

Judy Hasperis   Reno HS, Reno, NV

Tabbouleh

Serves: 4   *Lebanon*

1/2 cup olive oil
6 tablespoons fresh lemon juice
1/4 cup fresh mint, chopped
1/4 cup fresh parsley, chopped
3 green onions, chopped
1/2 teaspoon garlic, minced
3/4 teaspoon cumin
3/4 teaspoon salt
1/4 teaspoon black pepper
1 cup bulgar
1/2 cup pine nuts
2 medium tomatoes, finely chopped

Combine the dressing ingredients (olive oil, lemon juice, mint, parsley, green onions, garlic, cumin, salt, and pepper) and set aside. To the bulgar, add 1/2 cup boiling water and stir to moisten. Stir in the pine nuts, tomatoes, and the dressing ingredients. Chill for at least 8 hours or overnight.

Judy Hasperis   Reno HS, Reno, NV

Lamb & Lentil Stew

Serves: 4-6   *Persia*

1 cup lentils
1/4 cup olive oil
1 1/2 pounds stewing lamb or beef, cubed
1 small onion
3 carrots, peeled and cut into small sizes
4 small potatoes, peeled and cubed
1-2 tablespoons Better than Bullion
salt and pepper, to taste
ground cumin, to taste
3 cups water

Clean and rinse lentils, set to the side. Heat olive oil in a large pan, use medium to high flame and brown lamb cubes in small batches, salt & pepper to taste. Add lamb cubes, onions, carrots, lentils, potatoes, tomatoes, seasonings, bullion and water to the crock pot. Cook for 6- 8 hours. I prepare everything the night before and place it in a bowl. The next morning I place into crock pot, add water and leave for work.

"This recipe is delicious and a delightful change to the traditional beef stew dish. I first enjoyed this dish in Monterey, California and searched the net for one similar."

Yolanda Carlos   **Victor Valley HS, Victorville, CA**

Tabbouleh Salad

Serves: 6-8   *Saudi Arabia*

1 1/4 cups whole wheat couscous
1/2 cup boiling water
3 tablespoons olive oil
1 cucumber, peeled as desired, seeded, and diced to 1/2 inch
4 Roma tomatoes, seeded and diced to 1/2 inch
3 scallions, chopped
4 ounces Feta cheese, cubed or crumbled
1 (6 ounce) can sliced black olives, drained
3 tablespoons fresh Italian parsley, chopped
1 tablespoon mint, chopped
4 tablespoons fresh lemon juice
1/4 teaspoon salt (or less, because the olives and Feta add salty flavor)
pepper, to taste

Place couscous in a 3 quart mixing bowl. Pour boiling water over the couscous and cover the bowl with a lid or large plate. Let sit for 5 minutes. Fluff with a fork and gently fold in the olive oil. Once you have all the other ingredients chopped, add them into the couscous and continue to mix gently until all ingredients are distributed. Serve slightly warm or chill for 2 hours.

"If you add garbanzo beans or cannellini beans to this, you have a complete entreé that is heart healthy and loaded with fiber. Serve it on a bed of fresh spinach to add color."

Laurie Paolozzi   **West HS, Torrance, CA**

Lula Kabobs

Serves: 6-8   *Syria*

2 pounds ground beef or lamb or combination
1 large onion, finely chopped
1/4 cup bell pepper, finely chopped
1/4 cup fresh dill, chopped
1/2 teaspoon salt
1/4 teaspoon black pepper
1/4 teaspoon garlic powder

Heat barbecue or grill. Combine all ingredients until mixed well. Use about 1 cup of the mixture to form a "kabob" on a skewer, working and kneading until it stays in place. Repeat with remaining mixture. Grill kabobs until desired doneness.

"Serve with pita bread, buttered basmati rice and chopped green onion and cilantro. These can also be made into oblong patties instead of threading on skewers."

Laura de la Motte   **Turlock HS, Turlock, CA**

• •

Easy Beef Stroganoff
Serves: 4-6   ***Russia***

  1 pound beef fillet
  3 tablespoons butter
  1/4 cup onion, minced
  1/2 pound mushrooms, sliced
  1/4 teaspoon nutmeg
  salt and pepper, to taste
  3/4 cup sour cream
  egg noodles, cooked

Thinly slice beef into strips about 1 inch long. Melt 1 tablespoon of butter in pan and sauté the minced onion for about 2 minutes. Add the beef and sauté until the meat is evenly browned. Remove meat mixture from pan and keep warm. Add remaining butter to the pan, add mushrooms and sauté until soft. Add meat and onion mixture. Season with nutmeg, salt and pepper. Heat through. Remove from heat and stir in sour cream. Serve over noodles.

  "A family favorite. I sometimes slice the onion rather than mince for a different texture."
  Erna Slingland   **O'Brien MS, Reno, NV**

Beef Stroganoff with Egg Noodles
Serves: 4   ***Russia***

  1 pound of beef, thin sliced
  2 cloves garlic, finely minced
  2 tablespoons olive oil or butter
  1 yellow onion, juliennne
  1 cup mushrooms, crimini or button, sliced
  1/4 cup beef broth
  1/4 cup milk
  1 cup sour cream or yogurt
  dash dry mustard
  2 tablespoons dill, or more if you like it dilly!!
  1 tablespoons dry parsley
  1/2 teaspoon garlic salt
  salt and pepper, to taste
  2 cups egg noodles

Stroganoff: Sauté the onion in the fat until onions are translucent. Add the beef, garlic and mushrooms. Sauté until moisture has cooked off; there can be a bit of moisture in the pan, watch it closely. Add the stock. Sauté and reduce for 10 minutes. Add the milk, sour cream, mustard, dill and parsley. Heat but do not boil; it will curdle!! (Yuck) Reduce heat to keep warm. Add salt, pepper, garlic and dill, to taste. Serve over well-drained, cooked egg noodles. Noodles: In a large saucepan, boil 8 cups water with a splash of oil and salt. Add 2 cups of dry noodles. Cook about 13 minutes until they are al dente; firm, not mushy! Drain well. Want a bonus challenge? Make your own pasta.

"This is a easy fun family dinner. Reduce fat by using Greek yogurt.
Serve with some steamed green beans for a complete meal."

Priscilla Burns   **Pleasant Valley HS, Chico, CA**

Chicken Anastasia

Serves: 4   **Russia**

1 egg
1/4 cup milk
1/2 cup flour
1 teaspoon paprika
1/2 teaspoon salt
1/4 teaspoon pepper
4 boneless skinless chicken breast halves
2 tablespoons butter
2 tablespoons vegetable oil
2 medium cooking apples
2 tablespoons butter
4 ounces Swiss cheese, shredded
Sauce:
8 ounces fresh mushrooms, sliced
1 small onion, chopped
1 clove garlic
1/2 cup butter
1/2 teaspoon salt
1/4 teaspoon pepper
1 tablespoon flour
1 cup sour cream

Preheat oven to 350 degrees. Beat egg with milk in shallow bowl. On plate, combine flour with seasonings. Dredge chicken breast in seasoned flour, dip in egg mixture then back in flour mixture. Combine butter and oil in sauté pan; heat to melt butter. Cook coated chicken breast until golden brown on medium heat until cooked through. Remove and place in casserole dish, single layer. Sauté the apples in the butter until tender but not mushy. Arrange apple slices on top of chicken breast. Sauce: Sauté mushrooms, onion and garlic in butter until tender, about 10 minutes. Sprinkle with flour. Add salt and pepper and sauté until the flour has absorbed the fat. Add the sour cream and stir until the sauce is thick and creamy. Pour over the apple topped chicken pieces and sprinkle with the Swiss cheese. Bake for 45 minutes.

Janet Hough   **Foothill HS, Henderson, NV**

Maloshni Lopsha (Milk Noodles)

Serves: 12   **Russia**

3 quarts milk
1 pint half & half
1 1/2 teaspoons salt
1 teaspoon sugar
1 1/2 "chashki" noodles (about 2 1/2 large handfuls) or thin Jewish noodles

Using a 2 1/2 gallon double boiler, heat the milk and half & half till it forms bubbles. Do not let it boil. Now add the salt and sugar and stir well. Start adding the noodles, a handful at a time, stirring often. Simmer gently for 1/2 hour. Turn flame off and cover. Let stand in double boiler until it thickens (about 35-40 minutes) and serve.

"My Russian Molokan grandmother used to make this delicious creamy noodle soup."

Beth Gonzalez   **Bolsa Grande HS, Garden Grove, CA**

Russian Tea

Serves: 50-60   *Russia*

> 1/2 cup instant tea
> 2 cups Tang
> 2 1/2 cups sugar
> 1 1/2 cups dry lemonade mix
> 1 1/2 teaspoons cinnamon
> 1 1/2 teaspoons ground cloves

Combine all ingredients. Mix 1 heaping tablespoon in 8 ounces boiling water. Store in air tight container.

"I don't know if this is really from Russia, but it is delicious."

Joyce Gifford   **Desert Ridge HS, Mesa, AZ**

Scandinavia

●●●●●●●●●●●●●●●●●●●●●●●●●●●●●●●●●●●

Sandbakkels
Makes: 12   ***Denmark***

2 cups butter
1 1/2 cups sugar
2 eggs
1 teaspoon almond extract
5 cups flour
pinch of salt
metal tins or molds (approx. 3 inches x 1/2 inch)

Preheat over to 350 degrees. Cream butter and sugar. Add eggs and almond extract. Gradually add flour. Mix well. Form dough into small ball and press into mold. Place on baking sheet. Bake for 10 minutes.Remove molds from baking sheet and turn over to cool. Store in air tight container. Cool molds completely before placing cookie dough into mold again. Can be eaten plain or filled with fruit, whipped cream and berries.

"I have fond memories of making these at the holidays."

Renee Paulsin   **Hemet HS, Hemet, CA**

Fattingmann Cookies
Makes: a lot   ***Norway***

3 egg yolks
3 tablespoons sugar
3 tablespoons heavy cream
1 1/4 cups flour
powdered sugar

Beat egg yolks, add sugar and cream, beat well. Add flour and mix well to make a smooth dough. Roll out on a floured surface to 1/16 inch thickness. Cut in strips about 1 1/2 inches wide. Cut diagonally at 4 inch intervals. Make a 2 inch slit crosswise in the center and slip one end through the slit to make a "bow". Deep fry in hot lard (350 degrees) until delicately browned, about 1 1/2 minutes. Drain on paper towels. Cool and then dust with powdered sugar.

"My grandmother, Edith Knudson, immigrated to the United States from Norway.
These cookies were always a treat when she came to visit from Minnesota.
This recipes makes a lot of cookies if rolled to 1/16" thickness."

Wendy Duncan   **West Covina HS, West Covina, CA**

Norwegian Cookies (Rosettes)

Makes: 36-40   *Norway*

2 eggs
2 tablespoons sugar
1/4 teaspoon salt
1 teaspoon vanilla
1 cup milk
1 cup flour, sifted
vegetable or canola oil for frying

Whisk together eggs, sugar, salt, vanilla and milk. Add flour, beating until smooth. If time allows, refrigerate batter for 2 hours. (This step is not necessary but the rosettes will be crisper if the batter is allowed to rest.). Pour batter into a shallow square baking pan. Heat 2-3 inches of oil in a deep fryer or a large, heavy bottomed frying pan over medium-high heat to 365 degrees. Once the oil is up to temperature, submerge the rosette iron in the oil to heat it. Dip a rosette iron in the batter so that the batter covers the bottom and sides of the iron but not the top. Submerge the batter-covered iron in the hot oil, allowing the rosette to fry until golden brown. Remove iron and rosette from oil. Using a fork, slide rosette off of iron onto a paper towel-lined plate. Invert and cool. Sprinkle with powdered sugar, if desired. Store in an airtight container.

"Although my family is not Scandinavian, Grandma would often make a batch of rosettes during our family Christmas gatherings."

Renee Fertig   **North Monterey County HS, Castroville, CA**

Norwegian Red Rosemary Potatoes

Serves: 6   *Norway*

2 pounds red potatoes
1 teaspoon salt
1/3 cup butter
1/4 cup parsley, chopped
1/4 teaspoon basil or rosemary

Boil potatoes in water level 2 inches above the potatoes. Boil 12 to 15 minutes until tender. In a large fry pan, melt butter and add last two ingredients. Toss to coat. Serve immediately.

"My Grandfather has the Norway background. We often enjoyed these potatoes at our family gatherings."

Julie Eyre   **Alhambra HS, Alhambra, CA**

Pepparkakor Cookies

Makes: 3-4 dozen   *Sweden*

3 1/2 cups flour
2 teaspoons ginger
2 teaspoons cinnamon
2 teaspoons cloves
1 teaspoons baking soda
1/2 teaspoon salt
1 cup sugar
1 cup butter (do not use margarine)
1 egg
1/2 cup molasses

Sift together dry ingredients; set aside. Cream sugar and butter. Add egg and molasses. Stir in dry ingredients thoroughly. Refrigerate dough overnight for easy in handling. On a well-floured board, roll dough to 1/8 inch thickness. Cut into shapes, such as gingerbread people. Bake at 350 degrees for 10 minutes.

"These cookies are a favorite of my son, Martin, especially at Christmas."

Diane Castro   **Temecula Valley HS, Temecula, CA**

Swedish Apple Pie

Makes: 9 inch pie   *Sweden*

2 1/2 cups apples, peeled, cored, and sliced (enough to fill 2/3 of pie pan)
1 teaspoon ground cinnamon
1 teaspoon white sugar
1 cup white sugar
3/4 cup melted margarine or unsalted butter
1 cup all purpose flour
1 egg, lightly beaten
1 pinch of salt

Preheat oven to 350 degrees. Lightly grease 9 inch pie pan. Fill pan with sliced apples (about 2/3 of the way). Sprinkle with 1 teaspoon each of cinnamon and white sugar. Mix 1 cup of sugar with melted margarine. Stir in flour, egg and salt. Mix well and spread over apples. Bake for 60-65 minutes or until golden brown.

"My daughter-in-law is Swedish and this recipe is from her."

Carol Pellet   **Sowers MS, Huntington Beach, CA**

Swedish Klano

Serves: 6-8   *Sweden*

2 cups sugar
1 1/2 cubes margarine or butter
7 eggs
1 (12 ounce) can evaporated milk
2 teaspoons baking powder
1/2 cup brandy flavoring
2 teaspoons vanilla
flour (as needed)

In an extra large mixing bowl, cream sugar, margarine or butter. Add eggs and evaporated milk. Add flavoring and baking powder. While beating, start adding flour a cup at a time until you have a stiff and sticky dough. Put batter on a floured board and knead in small amounts of flour, being careful not to get too stiff of a dough. Roll out small amounts of dough on lightly floured board till it is just thick enough to cut into strips then triangles (pie dough thickness). Make a slit in the center of each triangle. Pull one end through center slit to form a twist. Fry in hot oil about 275 to 300 degrees, turning as they lightly brown. Remove and drain on paper towels. Drag each twist through powdered sugar or sugar and cinnamon, or leave some just plain. Let cool. Store in air tight containers. They get better with age! Great coffee dipping cookie like a biscotti.

Jennifer Templin   Cimarron-Memorial HS, Las Vegas, NV

Swedish Meat Loaf in Sour-Cream Pastry
Serves: 6-8   *Sweden*

Pastry:
1 teaspoon salt
2 1/4 cups flour
12 tablespoons chilled unsalted butter, cut up
1 egg
1/2 cup sour cream
1 tablespoon soft butter
Meat Filling:
4 tablespoons butter
3/4 cup mushrooms, finely chopped
3 pounds finely ground meat (beef, pork, ham, lamb, veal, or a combo)
1/3 cup onions, finely chopped
1/4 cup parsley, finely chopped
1 cup Swiss cheese, grated
1/2 cup milk
1 egg combined with 1 tablespoon milk

Preheat oven to 375 degrees. *Pastry:* Sift salt and flour together in large bowl. Cut in chilled butter. In a separate bowl, mix together egg and sour cream. Stir this into salt and flour mixture. Work into a dough, and roll into a soft, pliable ball. Cover and refrigerate for 1 hour. Divide dough in half, and roll into 2 rectangles large enough to line a loaf pan. Grease the loaf pan with the soft butter, and place one rectangle inside. *Meat Filling:* Melt butter in 10-12 inch pan. Sauté mushrooms until brown. Add ground meat and cook until done. Scrape meat and mushroom mixture into large bowl, and stir in chopped onions, parsley, cheese, and milk. Form into a football shape and place into loaf pan; lined with pastry. Place the second piece of pastry dough on top of meat loaf. Brush all edges of pastry with egg/milk mixture, and seal edges. Prick the top of pastry with fork to allow steam to escape. Bake for 45 minutes or until the loaf has turned golden brown. Serve thick slices of the hot meat loaf with dollops of sour cream and a side dish of lingonberries. (Lingonberries can be purchased at IKEA, but cranberries will work as well.)

"Meatloaf served with buttered carrots and mashed potatoes... my father's favorite meal. I made this recipe for him during one of his visits, with a nod to our Swedish heritage, and it quickly became his new favorite."

Charlene Nugent   Petaluma JHS, Petaluma, CA

Swedish Meatballs

Serves: 4-6   **Sweden**

1 pound ground beef
1/4 pound seasoned ground pork (Jimmy Dean in the roll is good.)
1 egg
1/4 teaspoon nutmeg
salt and pepper, to taste
1 cup half & half
1/2 cup cracker crumbs
1 onion, thinly sliced
1 (10.5 ounce) can cream of mushroom soup

Preheat oven to 350 degrees. Mix beef, pork, egg, nutmeg, salt and pepper together completely. Roll or scoop into bite-sized balls. Place meatballs on a non-greased baking sheet and bake for 10 minutes. Turn or roll balls over and continue to bake for another 10-15 minutes, until evenly browned. Place meatballs in a baking dish, cover with sliced onion and mushroom soup. Bake approximately 20 minutes, until sauce is bubbling. Meatballs can be fried instead of baked and the recipe can easily be doubled or tripled.

"This is always a family favorite and great at a buffet with the turkey and ham! It reminds me of great family gatherings."

Barbara Allen   Ayala HS, Chino Hills, CA

Swedish Rosettes

Serves: 24   **Sweden**

1 egg
1 teaspoons sugar
1/2 cup milk
1/2 cup flour
1/4 teaspoon salt
1 1/2 teaspoons lemon extract

Beat egg slightly. Add milk and sugar. Add flour and salt and mix until mixture is very smooth. (Should be about the consistency of heavy cream.) Add lemon extract. Pour batter into shallow pan (loaf pan is good). Place vegetable oil in an electric fryer and fill about 2/3 full and heat to 400 degrees. (I use an electric wok) Dip rosette irons* into the hot oil to heat them. Drain excess oil on paper towels. Dip heated forms into the batter to not more than 3/4 of their depth. Plunge the batter coated form into the hot oil and cook until active bubbling ceases. (Shake rosette iron while cooking) Rosette will usually fall off. If not, ease rosette off the iron with a fork and continue cooking until light brown. Lift rosettes out of the oil with a fork and drain on paper towels. While still warm, dip into powdered sugar. *Rosette irons are available at most kitchen stores.

"This is an all time favorite at our house. They are so easy, yet look so impressive! You will be surprised how many cookies you get with so few ingredients."

Linda A. Stokes   Riverton HS, Riverton, UT

Continued from page 32:

Chinese Pork Dumplings

...everything is well distributed. Keep cool in your refrigerator until you're ready to start folding. For wrappers, put the flour in a large bowl; stir in turmeric. Slightly beat egg, water and oil until combined; add to flour mixture. Use a wooden spoon to get the mixture well blended. If the dough is dry and cracking, add water, 1 tablespoon at a time until it's moist and springy. If the dough is sticky, add flour 1 tablespoon at a time until it's smooth. When the mixture has cooled a bit, knead it for about 7 minutes or until the dough becomes really elastic. Then cover the bowl in plastic wrap and refrigerate for about 30 minutes. After the dough has rested, use your thumb to poke a hole in the center. Gradually enlarge the hole until it looks like a large bagel. Using a sort of hand-over-hand technique, twist and pull the dough until it forms a rope about 3/4 inch in diameter. Slice the dough into pieces about 3/4 of an inch long, and roll each piece into a ball between your palms. On a well-floured work surface, roll out the ball into a thin disk about 3 inches in diameter, place a piece of parchment paper between the dough and the rolling pin will make things a bit easier. If you're not satisfied with the circles you're getting, use a cookie-cutter to trim them. Store the formed wrappers between sheets of parchment or waxed paper so that they don't dry out. Take a circle of dough, put 3/4 teaspoon of filling in the center, and fold dough in half to make half-moon shapes. Press the air out as you go and press or crimp the edges to seal. Lay the Napa cabbage leaves out on the base of a steamer and put the dumplings on them (dumplings will need to be cooked in batches and not all at once). Steam over medium-low heat for 10-12 minutes per batch or until the pork filling reaches internal temperature reaches 160 degrees F. Serve warm with a bit of soy sauce.

The Pork Council   PorkBeInspired.com

Index by Country

Taste OF THE WORLD

Index by Category

Index by Contributors

• •

Taste OF THE WORLD

Claiborne, Alice
Fairfield HS, Fairfield, CA 6

Clausen, Neva
Lebanon HS, Lebanon, OR................9, 56

Correia, Barbara
Foothill HS, Pleasanton, CA 80, 126

Curfman, Astrid
Newcomb Academy, Long Beach, CA 41, 44, 89

D

de la Motte, Laura
Turlock HS, Turlock, CA 58, 83, 123, 135

DeWitz, Donna
Oakmont HS, Roseville, CA............................21, 25

Dickerson, Kathleen
Colton HS, Colton, CA................................79, 87, 89

Diffenderfer, Leigh Ann
Newbury Park HS, Newbury Park, CA.............36, 50

Domeny, Scott
Del Oro HS, Loomis, CA 123

Duncan, Wendy
West Covina HS, West Covina, CA.................20, 139

E

Ebnit, Holly
Whittier Christian HS, La Habra, CA....................125

Enright, Jill
Granite Hills HS, El Cajon, CA 53

Ericksen, Julie
Skyline HS, Salt Lake City, UT 58, 107

Eyre, Julie
Alhambra HS, Alhambra, CA..................15, 42, 140

F

Farrell, Cherri
College Park HS, Pleasant Hill, CA 101, 120

Fertig, Renee
North Monterey County HS, Castroville, CA........140

Fossen, Doris
Sierra Vista JHS, Canyon Country, CA...................91

Fregulia, Maria
Lassen HS, Susanville, CA................................104

Freshour, Pat
Foothill HS, Palo Cedro, CA............................39, 62

Fullmer, Sue
ECTA, Las Vegas, NV 12, 24

Fuxa, Lori
Rancho Alamitos HS,
Garden Grove, CA................57, 66, 95, 113

G

Garrett, Su
Grace Yokley MS, Ontario, CA................11

Giauque, Laurie
Olympus HS, Salt Lake City, UT 73

Gifford, Joyce
Desert Ridge HS, Mesa, AZ 83, 138

Goldman, Dianne Lee
Cordova HS, Rancho Cordova, CA.................13, 133

Gonzalez, Beth
Bolsa Grande HS, Garden Grove, CA....................138

Guerrero, Beth
Selma HS, Selma, CA......................................8, 113

H

Haley, Laurel
Fresno HS, Fresno, CA 69

Harvey, Debbie
Amador Valley HS, Pleasanton, CA.................47, 76

Hasperis, Judy
Reno HS, Reno, NV................86, 133, 133

Hawes, Anne
Cottonwood HS, Murray, UT 92

Hawkins, Kris
Clovis West HS, Clovis, CA 41

Herndon, Peggy
Central Valley HS, Shasta Lake, CA.................41, 46

Hicks, Camille
Riverton HS, Riverton, UT 22, 23

Hobbs, Karyn
Lemoore HS, Lemoore, CA 125, 127

Hope, Sue
Lompoc HS, Lompoc, CA...........................74, 106

Hough, Janet
Foothill HS, Henderson, NV 7, 44, 46, 137

I

Ikkanda, Reiko
South Pasadena MS, South Pasadena, CA......38, 43

J

Johnson, Linda
Enochs HS, Modesto, CA.............................29, 56

Jolly, Shasta
Villa Park HS, Villa Park, CA 34, 60

K

Keane-Gruener, Mary
Carpinteria HS, Carpinteria, CA 90

154

For additional copies of *this* book,
and our *other* cookbook titles,
please visit our website:

www.creativecookbook.com

Or, use the re-order forms below.

 CREATIVE **ookbook** *Taste* OF THE WORLD

Please send me _____ copy(ies) of *Taste of the World* at **$12.00** ea.
(includes tax and shipping). Make checks payable to **Creative Cookbook Company.**
Mail this form with your check to: **6586 Colgate Avenue, Los Angeles, CA 90048**

Enclosed is my check for _____ book(s) at **$12.00** ea $_____.

Name _____

Address _____

City _____ State _____ Zip _____

CREATIVE **ookbook** *Taste* OF THE WORLD

Please send me _____ copy(ies) of *Taste of the World* at **$12.00** ea.
(includes tax and shipping). Make checks payable to **Creative Cookbook Company.**
Mail this form with your check to: **6586 Colgate Avenue, Los Angeles, CA 90048**

Enclosed is my check for _____ book(s) at **$12.00** ea $_____.

Name _____

Address _____

City _____ State _____ Zip _____